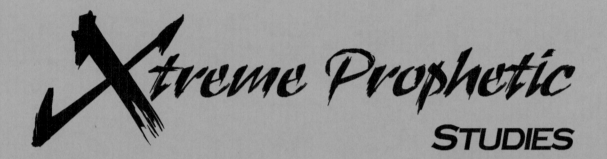

Xtreme Prophetic

STUDIES

One Module of the Apostolic Equipping Library
"Building Blocks for a Firm Foundation"

Unless otherwise noted, Scripture quotations are taken from the King James Version.

EXTREME PROPHETIC STUDIES

ISBN 1-886885-19-2

Published by Jonas Clark Ministries

A Great Commission Company

27 West Hallandale Beach Blvd., Hallandale Beach, FL 33009 www.jonasclark.com

Jonas Clark's products are available through most bookstores. To contact Jonas Clark Ministries directly call our Customer Care Department 954-456-4420. For easy online Internet orders visit www.jonasclark.com

Printed in the United States of America 01 02 03 04 05 – 05 04 03 02 01

Contents

Introduction

The subject of the prophetic ministry is so vast that no single work could discuss every surface of it. My intent with *Extreme Prophetic Studies* is to, by the grace of God, lay some foundational truths and boundaries that are solid enough to give those interested in the prophetic some firm points of balance.

Prophecy has always been a channel through which God has communicated with His people. Scripture declares that God spoke to the fathers at various times and in various ways through the prophets. (See Hebrews 1:1.)

The prophetic ministry is just as vital in New Testament times as it was in Old Testament times. The Apostle Paul validated prophecy in his letter to the church at Corinth, writing "Therefore, my brethren, desire earnestly to prophesy…" (1 Corinthians 14:39).

Indeed, Scripture declares that we are "built upon the foundation of the apostles and prophets, Jesus Christ himself being the chief corner stone" (Ephesians 2:20). Jesus Himself introduced a New Testament order of apostles, prophets, evangelists, pastors and teachers, all called to perfect the believer for the work of the ministry.

Because of this new order, the New Testament prophet, unlike the Old Testament prophet, is no longer the primary spokesman for God. Believers in any Spirit-filled local church can receive training, instruction and, most importantly, the unique and distinctive grace that rests on the five-fold ascension gifts to enable them to be effective in ministry, including prophetic utterances.

Throughout this workbook we focus on the New Testament ascension gift model of a prophet. We will also review the scope of prophecy itself, how to judge prophecy, the role of prophetic announcements and decrees, and the prophet's calling and training.

As we explore different aspects of the prophetic ministry, we will use the model of the New Testament ascension gift prophet as our guide, while also gleaning from Old Testament prophetic operations. We will also discover that the Holy Spirit is a prophetic Spirit and it is by His unction and His unction only that we prophesy.

We will learn that the strength of a prophet is his ability to hear, his revelation, and the appropriate release of utterance through his voice. Indeed, the essence of the prophetic is in the voice. Moses saw a bush, but he heard a voice. (See Acts 7:31-34.) John the Baptist was a voice crying in the wilderness. (See Matthew 3.) And Revelation 11 says that prophets will continue to play a major part in the Church until the end of the age.

Your partner in Christ,
Jonas Clark

"And Moses said unto him, Enviest thou for my sake? would God that all the LORD'S people were prophets, and that the LORD would put his spirit upon them!" (Numbers 11:29)

Chapter 1

FIVE FOLD ASCENSION GIFTS

The object of this lesson is to understand the different graces on the five-fold ascension gifts.

There are distinct and unique differences in the five-fold ascension gifts. All possess a different measure (*metron*) of grace. Let's begin our journey in the study of the five ascension gifts in this lesson. Notice the use of the word "some" and not "all" in the following text:

> "And he gave some, apostles; and some, prophets; and some, evangelists; and some, pastors and teachers; for the perfecting of the saints, for the work of the ministry, for the edifying of the body of Christ" (Ephesians 4:11-12).

In the above Scripture it is very clear that Jesus gave five different ascension gifts of apostles, prophets, evangelists, pastors, and teachers to the Body of Christ. If we do not understand the distinct differences and the role each plays in perfecting the Body of Christ, then it will be impossible for us to benefit from their uniquenesses.

For example, if we try to make a prophet function like a pastor, we abuse the prophet by trying to get him to do something that he is not called to do. Therefore, we cannot benefit from the unique grace on his life. Likewise, if we try to get a pastor to function like a prophet we abuse the pastor and cannot receive from the unique grace on his life.

It is extremely important that the Body of Christ thoroughly understand the differences between all five of the ascension gifts, thereby enabling us to advance and mature spiritually.

ALL FIVE ASCENSION GIFTS ARE UNIQUE

To better understand the differences between the five-fold ascension gifts, let's assign certain words that would best describe their unique functions. By looking at the words we generally associate with the different ascension gifts, we get a clearer idea of their distinctiveness. Also, let's list some short definitions of the five-fold ascension gifts as basic explanations of their *occupations* within the Body of Christ.

Let's start first with the ascension gift that we are the most familiar with, the pastor.

PASTOR *(poimen)*

Pastors are shepherds, called to love and nurture God's people.

> Words associated with pastor include shepherd, nurture, tend, feed, comfort, lead, protect, guard, sheep, nice, still waters, green pastures, patient, longsuffering, serve, counsel, and compassionate.

Pastors are wonderful gifts from Jesus and of great benefit to the local church. They are typically full of mercy, love and compassion. They offer wise counsel, sound godly wisdom and advice. There are many times when we need the loving grace and compassion that is on the pastoral ascension gift.

🔑 *The grace on the pastor is to impart in the believer a love for God's people.*

However, we need more than compassion and love, we also need to become disciples. For that we need the teacher. (Even though there is a unique ascension gift of teacher, it is not to say that the pastor cannot teach. See 1 Timothy 3:2).

TEACHER *(didaskalos)*

Teachers are set in the Body of Christ to instruct us in the Word of God.

> Words associated with the teacher include, explain, train, instruct, educate, simplify, academic, prepare, mature, tutor, expositor, disciple, steps, keys, and how to.

> Teachers have a unique grace to breakdown Scripture into easily understood and attainable steps. It is not enough for a person to only be born-again, they must be instructed in the Word of God and the ways of righteousness.

🔑 *The grace on the teacher is to impart a heart in the believer to make students of the Word of God.*

EVANGELISTS *(evaggelistes)*

Evangelism is telling the Good News that Jesus Christ died for sins, was raised from the dead on the third day, and is now extending forgiveness of sins to all who would believe.

> Words associated with the evangelist ascension gift include, go ye, souls, the lost, Gospel, Good News, herald, glad tidings, salvation, Great Commission, reconciliation, signs and wonders.

Without the ascension gift of the evangelist we would quickly forget about the Great Commission. The grace on the evangelist's gift is focused on the harvest. However, the evangelist's grace ends after a person is born again. Then that person needs the grace of the other ascension gifts to fully mature.

🔑 *The grace on the evangelist is to impart a heart in the believer for the lost.*

PROPHET *(prophetes)*

Prophets are ascension gifts that are set in the church to produce a hunger for the voice of God.

> Words associated with the prophet are see, hear, say, seer, mouthpiece, messenger, watchman, revelation, decree, proclaim, prepare the way, burden, announce, pray, utterances, turn, prophesy, prophecy, foretell, forthtell, root out, intercession, repentance, holiness, deliverance, dreams, and visions.

Prophets receive and communicate the mind and will of God. Jesus uses them to announce His will, unlock mysteries of His Word, bring conviction of sin, and focus the believer on an intimate spiritual and holy life. Prophets are spokesmen of God. The basic foundational function of a New Testament Prophet is for edification, exhortation and comfort.

🔑 *The grace on the prophet is to impart to the believer a hunger for the rhema Word of God (voice of God).*

APOSTLE *(apostolos)*

Apostles are God's builders (*architekton*) of the glorious church.

Words associated with the apostle are impart, confirm, activate, strengthen, strategies, the church, design, plan, structure, architect, ordain, reform, proton, demand, builder, doctrine, administrate, father, govern, pioneer, trailblazer, foundation, sent-one, warrior, first, order, messenger, and ambassador.

Apostles are the most panoramic of the five-fold ascension gifts. They have the ability to see the whole picture. Whereas a pastor might be more local church-minded, the apostle has more of a world (universal) church vision. His heart is to mobilize the local church into a fine-tuned, invading and occupying army.

The grace on the apostle is to impart to the believer a heart to build Jesus's Church.

All of these words best describe the different attributes of the various ascension (*doma*) gifts. Once we understand their differences we can benefit from their uniquenesses.

A FULL-TIME VOCATION

Five-fold ascension gifts are full-time ministry vocations set in the Body of Christ to thoroughly prepare every believer for the work of the ministry. The work of the ministry is...

√ The Great Commission.

√ Serving and meeting the needs of others.

√ Doing the work of the apostle, prophet, evangelist, pastor, and teacher.

"I therefore, the prisoner of the Lord, beseech you that ye walk worthy of the *vocation* wherewith ye are called" (Ephesians 4:1, Emphasis added).

In the Scripture above, the Apostle Paul specifically speaks to the five-fold ascension gifts about their calling. He tells them to "walk (live) worthy of their vocation."

The word vocation is a Latin word meaning "calling." The English definition of the word *vocation* means "regular occupation."

When we look at the five-fold ascension gifts as "regular occupations" rather than part-time activities, it provides us with clear insight into the difference between the believer and the five-fold ascension gift.

Five-fold ascension gifts are set in the Body of Christ and the local church specifically as "full time vocations." Their call is to impart the unique grace that is on their life into every believer. Every local church should have resident in the believers of that local church all five graces of apostles, prophets, evangelists, pastors, and teachers.

NOT EVERYONE IS AN ASCENSION GIFT

Not everybody in the local church is called into full-time ascension gift ministry. This does not mean that you, the born again believer, are not called into ministry. In fact, every five-fold ascension gift is called to provide a unique grace for you to be thoroughly equipped to do the work of the ministry.

Some think that they must be a five-fold ascension gift to qualify for ministry. This is not the case. Let's explain:

√ It is possible to pastor, nurture, love, care for, and comfort others without being an ascension gift pastor. Yet, to do so effectively, as a believer, you need the unique grace of an ascension gift pastor imparted to you.

√ It is possible to teach the Word of God and not be an ascension gift teacher. Yet, to raise up a disciple of Christ effectively you need, as a believer, the unique grace of the ascension gift teacher imparted to you.

√ It is possible to lead someone to Jesus through sharing the Gospel and not be an ascension gift evangelist. Yet, to have a heart for the lost requires an impartation of the five-fold ascension gift evangelist into your life.

√ It is possible to prophesy and not be an ascension gift prophet. Yet, to create a heart in the believer that hungers for the rhema word of God (voice of God) you need the unique grace of the prophet imparted to you.

√ You can have a desire to build the local church and not be an ascension gift apostle. Yet, to have a desire to build the local church you need the grace of the ascension gift apostle imparted to you.

A person does not have to be a car to enjoy the benefits of a car. Nor does a person have to be an airplane to enjoy the benefits of an airplane. Likewise, a believer does not have to be a five-fold ascension gift of apostle, prophet, evangelist, pastor, or teacher to benefit from the unique grace on the life of those different ascension gifts. The believer is enabled to become complete only after the impartation of all five-fold ascension gifts in his or her life.

When we understand that every born again believer can draw upon the unique grace of all five ascension gifts to be thoroughly equipped for the work of the ministry, this gives us a great wholeness and a proper perspective of ministry.

Finally, what is the work of the ministry that the believer is being equipped for? It is the work of the apostle (build), prophet (prophesy), evangelists (reach the lost), pastor (love God's people), and teacher (make disciples) that has been imparted to that believer from all five ascension gifts.

APERCU

There are distinct and unique differences in the five-fold ascension gifts.

Pastors are shepherds, called to love and nurture God's people.

Teachers are set in the Body of Christ to instruct us in the Word of God.

Prophets are ascension gifts that are set in the church to produce a hunger for the voice of God.

Apostles are God's builders (*architekton*) of the glorious church.

The English definition of the word "vocation" means "regular occupation."

The work of the ministry is the work of the apostle (build), prophet (prophesy), evangelists (reach the lost), pastor (love God's people), and teacher (make disciples) that has been imparted to the believer from all five ascension gifts.

Reflect & Apply

FIVE-FOLD ASCENSION GIFTS

1. There are distinct and _____ in the five-fold ascension gifts.

2. By looking at the words we generally associate with the different ascension gifts, we get a clearer idea of their _____.

3. Apostles are called to impart in every believer a heart to _____ God's Church.

4. Prophets are ascension gifts set in the church to produce a hunger for the _____ _____ of God.

5. _____ is telling the Good News that Jesus Christ died for sins, was raised from the dead, and is now extending forgiveness of sins to all who would believe.

6. Pastors are _____ called to impart into the heart of the believer a love for God's people.

7. Teachers are set in the Body of Christ to impart a heart in every believer to _____ _____ others in the Word of God.

8. What does the grace on the pastor impart to the believer?

_____

_____

9. What does the grace on the teacher impart to the believer?

_____

_____

10. What does the grace on the evangelist impart to the believer?

_____

_____

11. What does the grace on the prophet impart to the believer?

_____

_____

12. What does the grace on the apostle impart to the believer?

_____

_____

13. The English definition of the word "vocation" means _____.

14. How many ascension gifts did Jesus give to every believer in His church?

_____

15. What is the work of the ministry that the believer is being equipped for? Explain.

_____

_____

_____

NOTES

Chapter 2

ALL CAN PROPHESY

In this lesson we learn that it is God's will that all should prophesy.

"Follow after charity, and desire spiritual gifts, but rather that ye may prophesy" (1 Corinthians 14:1).

The prophet is called into ministry by God's sovereign will alone. Jesus Christ calls the five-fold ascension gift prophet, and prophecy is from the Holy Spirit. Not everyone is a prophet. Scripture specifically declares that God gave some apostles, some prophets, some evangelists, some pastors and teachers. (See Ephesians 4:11.) However, everyone who is born again and baptized in the Holy Spirit can enter a measure of the prophetic dimension.

Most people understand that the initial evidence of being baptized by the Holy Spirit is speaking in other tongues. Many Spirit-filled Christians, however, do not understand that when they are baptized in the Holy Spirit they are also empowered to prophesy. In fact, the realm of prophetic utterance should be as natural to the Spirit-filled believer as speaking in other tongues. The reason it is not is either because of a lack of Scriptural understanding and/or religious resistance.

SONS AND DAUGHTERS SHALL PROPHESY

The Apostle Peter preached his first sermon just after leaving the Upper Room, where the Holy Spirit baptized him. In his sermon he spoke about the manifestation of the Holy Spirit that the people were seeing and hearing. He boldly declared,

> "But this is that which was spoken by the prophet Joel; and it shall come to pass in the last days, saith God, I will pour out of my Spirit upon all flesh: and your sons and your daughters shall prophesy, and your young men shall see visions, and your old men shall dream dreams: And on my servants and on my handmaidens I will pour out in those days of my Spirit; and they shall prophesy" (Acts 2:16-18).

Notice how Apostle Peter connected the outpouring of the Holy Spirit to prophecy. Today, some have connected the outpouring of the Holy Spirit only with speaking in other tongues. Let's look at another example.

PROPHETIC BELIEVERS IN EPHESUS

When the Apostle Paul went to Ephesus he met 12 disciples who never heard about the baptism of the Holy Spirit. They were bona fide believers, yet had never entered the supernatural realm of the Spirit of God; born again, but not filled with the Spirit. Paul first responded to their lack of understanding about the gift of the Holy Spirit, then, after a short teaching, laid his hands on them. The Holy Ghost filled them and the evidence was that they spoke in other tongues and prophesied. Let's read what he said.

> "He said unto them, have ye received the Holy Ghost since ye believed? And they said unto him, we have not so much as heard whether there be any Holy Ghost. And he said unto them, unto what then were ye baptized? And

they said, Unto John's baptism. Then said Paul, John verily baptized with the baptism of repentance, saying unto the people, that they should believe on him, which should come after him, that is, on Christ Jesus. When they heard this, they were baptized in the name of the Lord Jesus. And when Paul had laid his hands upon them, the Holy Ghost came on them; and they spake with tongues, and prophesied" (Acts 19:2-6).

Notice that they were baptized in the Holy Ghost with the manifestation of speaking in other tongues and prophecy. There were no seminars, conferences or teaching materials provided for their prophetic development. Prophecy simply happened as a result of the baptism in the Holy Spirit. It is the same today. If you are born again, and filled with the Holy Spirit, you are positioned for prophecy.

CHILDREN PROPHESY

- Joel 2:28-29; Psalm 8:2

WOMEN PROPHESY

Women can prophesy and be prophets. Here are a few examples:

- Miriam (Exodus 15:20)
- Deborah (Judges 4:4)
- Huldah (2 Kings 22:14; 2 Chronicles 34:22)
- Isaiah's wife (Isaiah 8:3)
- Anna (Luke 2:36)
- Sons and daughters… men and women (Acts 2:17-18)
- Philips four daughters (Acts 21:9)
- Women in the Corinthian church (1 Corinthians 11:5)
- Jezebel (a false prophetess; Revelation 2:20)

DESIRE TO PROPHESY

The Word of God teaches us that we should desire to prophesy. Let's take a closer look at this very revealing Scripture.

> "<u>Follow after charity, and desire spiritual gifts, but rather that ye may prophesy.</u> For he that speaketh in an unknown tongue speaketh not unto men, but unto God: for no man understandeth him; howbeit in the spirit he speaketh mysteries. But he that prophesieth speaketh unto men to edification, and exhortation, and comfort" (1 Corinthians 14:1-3, Emphasis added).

The word "desire" comes from the Greek word *zeloo*, meaning to "burn with zeal." It is important to point out that it is unquestionably Scriptural for a believer to desire to prophesy.

Notice the high level of significance that the Holy Spirit Himself places on prophecy. To desire also means...

- wish for

- long for

- want

- pursue strongly

- possess a passion for

- covet

- crave

- can't live without

- unsatisfied without.

For every believer to desire (*zeloo*) to prophesy is completely Scriptural and emphasized by the Holy Spirit.

- Moses validated prophecy for every believer.

"And Moses said unto him, Enviest thou for my sake? <u>would God that all the LORD'S people were prophets</u>, and that the LORD would put his spirit upon them!" (Numbers 11:29, Emphasis added)

- Other Scriptures also encourage prophecy.

    "Follow after charity, and desire spiritual gifts, but rather that ye may prophesy" (1 Corinthians 14:1).

    "I would that ye all spake with tongues, but rather that ye prophesied: for greater is he that prophesieth than he that speaketh with tongues, except he interpret, that the church may receive edifying" (1 Corinthians 14:5).

    "Wherefore, brethren, covet to prophesy, and forbid not to speak with tongues" (1 Corinthians 14:39).

PURPOSE OF PROPHECY

The three most significant purposes of prophecy are edification, exhortation and comfort.

"But he that prophesieth speaketh unto men to edification, and exhortation, and comfort" (1 Corinthians 14:3, Emphasis added).

1. The word "edification" comes from the Greek word *oikodome*, meaning "to build up, establish, strengthen, to make effective." (See 1 Corinthians 14:3-4.)

2. The word "exhortation" comes from the Greek word *paraklesis*, meaning "a comforting encouragement provided in times of disappointment and affliction resulting in strengthening the resolve of the believer." (See 2 Chronicles 5:8; 1 Corinthians 14:3; Acts 16:32.)

3. The word "comfort" comes from the Greek word *paramuthia*, meaning "to provide a freedom from worry during times of grief, affliction or distress and bringing assurance to the believer." (See 1 Corinthians 14:3; Isaiah 40:1-2.)

- Prophecy edifies both believers and the local church. (See 1 Corinthians 14:4, 12, 17, 19.)

APERCU

Not everyone is a prophet.

Everyone who is born again and baptized in the Holy Spirit can enter a measure of the prophetic dimension. (See 1 Corinthians 14:1; Romans 12:4.)

The realm of prophetic utterance should be as common in churches as speaking in other tongues.

Peter connected the outpouring of the Holy Spirit to prophecy.

When Paul laid his hands on the believers in Ephesus they spoke in other tongues and prophesied. (See Acts 19:2-6.)

The Word of God teaches us to desire to prophesy.

The word "edification" comes from the Greek word *oikodome*, meaning "to build up, establish, strengthen, to make effective."

The word "exhortation" comes from the Greek word *paraklesis*, meaning "a comforting encouragement provided in times of disappointment and affliction resulting in strengthening the resolve of the believer."

The word "comfort" comes from the Greek word *paramuthia*, meaning "to provide a freedom from worry during times of grief, affliction or distress and bringing assurance to the believer."

Reflect & Apply

ALL CAN PROPHESY

1. The prophet is called into ministry by God's _____.

2. Everyone who is born again and baptized in the Holy Spirit can enter a measure of the
_____.

3. What did the Apostle Peter preach about in his first sermon after leaving the Upper Room?
_____

4. What did the Apostle Peter connect the outpouring of the Holy Spirit to? _____
_____

5. What happened to the believer that the Apostle Paul met in Ephesus? (Acts 19:2-6)
Explain. _____
_____
_____
_____
_____
_____

6. What two signs made it evident that the believers in Ephesus had been filled by the Holy Spirit?

1._____

2._____

7. Name three women prophets in the Bible.

1._____

2._____

3._____

8. What spiritual gift is every believer commanded to desire? (1 Corinthians 14:1-3)

_____

9. What does the Greek word *zeloo* mean?

_____

10. Moses _____ prophecy for every believer. (Numbers 11:29)

11. Name the three most significant purposes of prophecy.

1._____

2._____

3._____

12. What does the Greek word *oikodome* mean? (1 Corinthians 14:3-4)

_____

_____

NOTES

_____

_____

_____

_____

_____

_____

_____

_____

_____

_____

_____

_____

_____

_____

_____

_____

_____

_____

NOTES

GIFT OF PROPHECY

In this lesson we will study the nine gifts of the Holy Spirit, paying particular attention to the utterance gifts and the simple gift of prophecy.

TWO TYPES OF PROPHECY

There are two types of prophecy: forthtelling and foretelling.

- Forthtelling prophecy, the simple gift of prophecy, is an inspired declaration of the divine will and purpose of God. It is inspired, but not predictive. Its primary use is for edification, exhortation and comfort.

- Foretelling prophecy, however, is predictive (speaking of things to come) and directive in it message.

NINE GIFTS OF THE HOLY SPIRIT

Before we look at the gift of prophecy (forthtelling) let's examine the nine gifts of the Spirit. The nine gifts of the Holy Spirit can be grouped into three categories: the power gifts, the revelation gifts and the utterance gifts.

The power gifts do something. The revelation gifts know something. The utterance gifts say something.

> "For to one is given by the Spirit the word of wisdom; to another the word of knowledge by the same Spirit; To another faith by the same Spirit; to another the gifts of healing by the same Spirit; To another the working of miracles; to another prophecy; to another discerning of spirits; to another divers kinds of tongues; to another the interpretation of tongues" (1 Corinthians 12:8-10).

POWER GIFTS (*gifts that do something*)

1.   **Gift of Faith** – a supernatural faith outside of our human will that empowers us to believe for the impossible.

2.   **Gifts of Healing** – the healing power of God demonstrated through the manifestation of various healings.

3.   **Gift of the Working of Miracles** – seen when the laws of nature are interpreted; time stood still for Joshua, Moses parted the Red Sea, Elijah ran faster than Ahab's chariot, and Jesus turned water into wine, etc.

Most events are a combination of the gifts of the Spirit working together. For example, Elijah's ax head that floated is the gift of faith coupled with the gift of the working of miracles. (See 2 Kings 6:1-7.)

REVELATION GIFTS (*gifts that know something*)

1.   **Gift of the Word of Wisdom** – Prophecies that speak of the future. (See John 14:29.)

2.   **Gift of the Word of Knowledge** – Prophecies that speak of now and the past, e.g. the woman at the well. (See John 4:18.)

3.   **Gift of the Discerning of Spirits** – Reveals the spirit that's working; Holy Spirit, demon spirit, or human spirit.

A word of wisdom or a word of knowledge is only a short fragment of divine prophetic information. These utterance gifts reveal information that would be impossible to know without the Holy Spirit making it known.

All the gifts of the Holy Spirit are given out according to His will. "But all these worketh that one and the selfsame Spirit, dividing to everyman severally as he will" (1 Corinthians 12:11).

One cannot make the gifts of the Holy Spirit manifest according to his or her will apart from the Holy Spirit. The Holy Spirit does, however, want the believer to yield to Him in faith. (See Romans 12:6.)

UTTERANCE GIFTS (*gifts that say something*)

1.   **Gift of Prophecy** – The Gift of Prophecy has no foretelling revelation in it. It speaks to men to edification, exhortation and comfort. (See 1 Corinthians 14:3.) If prophecy (foretelling) doesn't build up, strengthen or comfort, it's not prophecy.

2.   Gift of Tongues – The Gift of Tongues is not to be confused with a man's spirit talking to God in an inarticulate language. (See 1 Corinthians 14:14.) This gift is demonstrated in the local church assembly when God wants to edify the local church. It is an utterance in an unknown tongue.

3.   Gift of Interpretation of Tongues – When the Gift of Tongues is coupled with the Gift of the Interpretation of Tongues, it equals prophecy and the church is built up.

SIMPLE GIFT OF PROPHECY

The simple gift of prophecy (forthtelling) is one of the three utterance gifts. Of these three utterance gifts, prophecy is the most important because it edifies the local church.

•   It takes both the gift of tongues and the gift of interpretation of tongues to equal prophecy. Tongues alone are not considered to be prophetic unless they are coupled with an interpretation.

•   All believers who are baptized in the Holy Ghost can speak in other tongues to edify themselves. (See 1 Corinthians 14:14.)

•   The gift of tongues, however, is most often seen in local church assemblies. During a break or an appropriate time during a local church service one may be heard with a different sounding unknown tongue coming forth. The sound is often very authoritarian and a reverent hush will fall on those who hear it.

•   Another believer standing by may interpret the unknown tongue (see 1 Corinthians 14:27) or the same person who brought forth the unknown tongue may interpret it. (See 1 Corinthians 14:13).

- The gift of prophecy is a supernatural utterance in a known tongue. The gift of tongues is a supernatural utterance in an unknown tongue.

- To prophesy means to flow forth or to bubble forth like a fountain, and to speak.

- One who prophecies will deliver the mind, will and purpose of the Lord into our lives.

The simple gift of prophecy (forthtelling) always edifies. We must be careful not to confuse the simple gift of prophecy with the ascension gift ministry of a prophet. The fact that someone prophesies does not make him or her a five-fold ascension gift prophet. Anyone can prophesy according to 1 Corinthians 14:31.

When a prophet prophesies, he will also have at least two, if not all three of the revelation gifts in operation in his life. Again, the three revelation gifts are: word of knowledge, word of wisdom, and the discerning of spirits.

APERCU

There are two types of prophecy: forthtelling and foretelling.

The power gifts do something. The revelation gifts know something. The utterance gifts say something.

A word of wisdom or a word of knowledge is only a short fragment of divine prophetic information.

All the gifts of the Holy Spirit are given out according to His will. "But all these worketh that one and the selfsame Spirit, dividing to everyman severally as he will" (1 Corinthians 12:11).

It takes both tongues and interpretation of tongues to equal prophecy.

All believers who are baptized in the Holy Ghost can speak in other tongues to edify themselves. (See 1 Corinthians 14:14.)

The simple gift of prophecy has no foretelling revelation in it.

NOTES

_____

_____

_____

_____

_____

_____

_____

_____

_____

_____

_____

_____

_____

_____

_____

_____

_____

_____

Reflect & Apply

GIFT OF PROPHECY

1. What are the two types of prophecy? _____
_____

2. Of the two types of prophecy which one is called the simple gift of prophecy?
_____
_____

3. Describe forthtelling prophecy.
_____
_____
_____
_____

4. Name the three categories that the nine gifts of the Holy Spirit can be grouped in.

  1._____

  2._____

  3._____

5. What must prophecy do in order to be true prophecy? (1 Corinthians 14:3)

_____

_____

6. The simple gift of prophecy (forthtelling) is one of the three _____ gifts.

7. What two gifts of the Holy Spirit equal prophecy?

    1._____

    2. _____

8. The simple gift of prophecy (forthtelling) always _____.

9. Anyone can prophesy according to what Scripture?

_____

10. Name three of the utterance gifts of the Holy Spirit.

    1._____

    2. _____

    3. _____

NOTES

PROPHETS AND PROPHECY

In this lesson we discuss the essence of prophecy and its purpose.

THE PROPHETIC CALLING

The simplest definition of a prophet is one who is a mouthpiece for God.

> The ascension gift prophet is a gift that the Lord Jesus Himself set in the Church. "He gave some apostles, some prophets…" (Ephesians 4:11).

> The gift of prophecy is given to the Church by the Holy Spirit Himself, who distributes His gifts "to each one individually just as He wills" (1 Corinthians 12:11).

> Prophecy is called a gift of the Holy Spirit.

Jesus gave prophets, the Holy Spirit gave prophecy.

Specific prophets mentioned in the New Testament include, Agabus, Judas, Silas and John. (See Acts 11:28; 15:32; Revelation 10:8-11.) There were also prophets at the Antioch church. (See Acts 13:1.) The four daughters of Philip are not specifically called prophets but did prophesy. (See Acts 21:9.) Barnabas is sometimes thought of as a prophet, but more probably was an apostle with a prophetic gift.

Some prophets were called from birth like Jeremiah (see Jeremiah 1:4-5) and John the Baptist (see Luke 1:15-16). Amos, however, just had a powerful experience with God who called him while tending his flocks. (See Amos 7:14-15.)

⌐—• God alone uniquely calls each prophet.

Prophets should have a passion for God Himself that is evident in an intimate and corporate prayer life. The prophet should also have a heart for God's people that is visible in the prophet's love for them (see 1 Corinthians 13:2; Matthew 22:40) and a resolve for building the local church. (See 1 Corinthians 14:12.)

WHAT IS PROPHECY?

Prophecy is the Word of God spoken from the mouth of men. Scriptural references include:

> "I will raise them up a Prophet from among their brethren, like unto thee, and will put my words in his mouth; and he shall speak unto them all that I shall command him" (Deuteronomy 18:18).

> "And I have put my words in thy mouth…" (Isaiah 51:16).

> "Then the Lord put forth his hand, and touched my mouth. And the Lord said unto me, behold, I have put my words in thy mouth" (Jeremiah 1:9).

HOW DOES PROPHECY COME ABOUT?

1. Prophecy comes after a divine unction or urging from the Holy Spirit to prophesy.

Scripture says, "Knowing this first that no prophecy of the scripture is of any private interpretation. <u>For the prophecy came not in old time by the will of man: but holy men of God spake as they were moved by the Holy Ghost</u>" (2 Peter 1:20-21, Emphasis added).

- The word "moved" comes from the Greek word *phero*, meaning "to bring forth or to bubble up."

2. Prophecy comes about during times of worship.

"Now there were in the church that was at Antioch certain prophets and teachers; as Barnabas, and Simeon that was called Niger, and Lucius of Cyrene, and Manaen, which had been brought up with Herod the tetrarch, and Saul. <u>As they ministered to the Lord</u>, and fasted, the Holy Ghost said, Separate me Barnabas and Saul for the work whereunto I have called them. And when they had fasted and prayed, and laid their hands on them, they sent them away. So they, being sent forth by the Holy Ghost, departed unto Seleucia; and from thence they sailed to Cyprus" (Acts 13:1-4, Emphasis added).

3. Prophecy comes through faith.

"Having then gifts differing according to the grace that is given to us, whether prophecy, <u>let us prophesy according to the proportion of faith</u>" (Romans 12:6, Emphasis added).

4. Prophecy comes when the Spirit of God comes on you.

"And the Spirit of the LORD will come upon thee, and thou shalt prophesy with them, and shalt be turned into another man."

"And it was so, that when he had turned his back to go from Samuel, God gave him another heart: and all those signs came to pass that day. "And when they came thither to the hill, behold, a company of prophets met him; and the <u>Spirit of God came upon him, and he prophesied among them</u>" (1 Samuel 10:6, 9-10, Emphasis added).

"But this is that which was spoken by the prophet Joel; And it shall come to pass in the last days, saith God, I will pour out of my Spirit upon all flesh: and your sons and your daughters shall prophesy, and your young men shall see visions, and your old men shall dream dreams: And on my servants and on my handmaidens I will pour out in those days of my Spirit; and they shall prophesy" (Acts 2:16-18).

All should stir up the gift:

"Wherefore I put thee in remembrance that thou stir up the gift of God, which is in thee by the putting on of my hands" (2 Timothy 1:6).

Examples of prophecy through song: See Exodus 15, Judges 5, Revelation 15, 1 Corinthians 14:15.

At times a great compulsion to prophesy is felt:

"The lion hath roared, who will not fear? the Lord GOD hath spoken, who can but prophesy?" (Amos 3:8)

"Then I said, I will not make mention of him, nor speak any more in his name. But his word was in mine heart as a burning fire shut up in my bones, and I was weary with forbearing, and I could not stay" (Jeremiah 20:9, Emphasis added).

Prophets never lose control of themselves:

"And the spirits of the prophets are subject to the prophets" (1 Corinthians 14:32).

THE SOURCE OF ALL PROPHECY

Prophetic messages can be traced to three sources.

1.   The Holy Spirit (See 2 Peter 1:21.)

2.   The human spirit (See Jeremiah 23:17.)

3.   An evil spirit (See Jeremiah 23:13.)

JUDGING PROPHECY

All prophecy should be judged. To judge prophecy means we use the logos of the Word of God as our final guide to the accuracy of any prophetic utterance. Remember, the Holy Spirit never contradicts Himself. Some Scriptural references for judging prophecy include:

- "Beloved, believe not every spirit, but try the spirits whether they are of God: because many false prophets are gone out into the world" (1 John 4:1).

🔑 The word "try" means to put to the test for Scriptural accuracy.

- "Let the prophets speak two or three, and let the other judge" (1 Corinthians 14:29).

- The Apostle Paul submitted his revelation and doctrine for judgment. (See Galatians 1:11-2:2.)

- "Quench not the Spirit. Despise not prophesyings. Prove all things; hold fast that which is good" (1 Thessalonians 5:19-21).

We should never be intimidated or afraid of prophets because they utter God's good thoughts toward us.

10 KEYS FOR JUDGING PROPHECY

The following is a list of 10 keys for judging the accuracy of prophetic words.

1. **Does the prophetic message violate the written Word of God?**

   The Holy Spirit will never violate, in word, deed, or spirit, the logos i.e., the Scriptures. Does the prophecy agree with the letter and the spirit of the Scriptures?

2. **Does the prophetic message give glory to Jesus Christ?**

Speaking of the ministry of the Holy Spirit, Jesus said, "He shall glorify Me; for He shall take of Mine, and shall disclose it to you" (John 16:14).

"Wherefore I give you to understand, that <u>no man speaking by the Spirit of God calleth Jesus accursed:</u> and that no man can say that Jesus is the Lord, but by the Holy Ghost" (1 Corinthians 12:3, Emphasis added).

"By this you know the Spirit of God: every spirit that confesses that Jesus Christ has come in the flesh is from God" (1 John 4:2).

The purpose of all prophecy should be that "in all things God may be glorified through Jesus Christ" (1 Peter 4:11).

3.   Is the prophetic word ambiguous?

Does the prophetic message mean anything? "The Spirit speaketh expressly" (1 Timothy 4:1). A true prophetic word has understandable meaning. Even though we see through a glass darkly, God is perfectly capable of making Himself clear.

4.   Does the prophetic word lead you closer to Jesus or toward idolatry?

Scripture is clear. Even if a prophecy is presented with signs and wonders coming to pass, if it causes you to "go after other gods" it is not from the Lord.

"If there arise among you a prophet, or a dreamer of dreams, and giveth thee a sign or a wonder, And the sign or the wonder come to pass, whereof he spake unto thee, saying, Let us go after other gods, which thou hast not known, and let us serve them; Thou shalt not hearken unto the words of that prophet, or that dreamer of dreams: for the LORD your God proveth you, to know whether ye love the LORD your God with all your heart and with all your soul" (Deuteronomy 13:1-3).

5.   **Do the prophecies produce liberty or bondage? Do they instill fear and discouragement?**

"And, lo, I perceived that God had not sent him; but that he pronounced this prophecy against me: for Tobiah and Sanballat had hired him. Therefore was he hired, that I should be afraid, and do so, and sin, and that they might have matter for an evil report, that they might reproach me" (Nehemiah 6:12-13, Emphasis added).

6.   **Does your spirit bear witness with the prophetic message?**

One should have an inner-witness knowing that the prophecy is accurate. "But you have an unction from the Holy One, and you know all things" (1 John 2:20).

7.   **Have you let trusted mature leaders review the prophecy with you?**

"Obey them that have the rule over you, and submit yourselves: for they watch for your souls, as they that must give account, that they may do it with joy, and not with grief: for that is unprofitable for you" (Hebrews 13:17, Emphasis added).

8.   Does the prophecy edify, exhort, comfort?

All prophecy should bring encouragement and comfort. If it doesn't, then it's not prophecy.

9.   Does the prophetic messenger live the Christian life?

Ask yourself these questions as you judge the prophecy:

- Should I trust the prophecies of someone living in sin?

- Is this prophet living in sin?

- Is the fruit of the Spirit evident in the person's life? (See Matthew 7:15.)

- What kind of prophetic track record does this person have?

- Is this person living in rebellion? (None of these questions involved judging the persons salvation.)

10.   Does the prophecy come true?

"And if thou say in thine heart, How shall we know the word which the LORD hath not spoken? When a prophet speaketh in the name of the LORD, if the thing follow not, nor come to pass, that is the thing which the LORD hath not spoken, but the prophet hath spoken it <u>presumptuously</u>: thou shalt not be afraid of him" (Deuteronomy 18:21-22, Emphasis added).

PROPHECY CAN BE CONDITIONAL

There are many "if" statements coupled with the prophetic word.

- God didn't destroy Nineveh because they repented after the prophetic word of Jonah. (See Jonah 1:1, 3:4-10.)

- Hezekiah's life was extended by 15 years. (See 2 Kings 20:1-6.)

NOT A SIGN OF SPIRITUALITY

Prophecy is not a sign of spirituality or one's special position with God.

We should never get caught up or mesmerized by prophets or prophecy. Beware of giving prominence to prophets who met with or prophesied to the president, governor, mayor, etc. Just because they had a meeting with or a prophetic word for someone in authority or some celebrity doesn't give them credibility! Always judge what was said.

- Baby Christians can prophesy. (See Acts 19:5-7.)

- Caiphus, who condemned Jesus, prophesied. (See John 11:49-52.)

- Demon-possessed Saul prophesied. (See 1 Samuel 16:14, 18:10, 19:9.)

- A demon-inspired damsel prophesied. (See Acts 16:16.)

- Even a donkey can prophesy if God wants to use it.
  (See Numbers 22:28-33.)

GUIDELINES FOR PROPHECY DURING CHURCH SERVICES

Certain guidelines are set forth in Scripture concerning the operation of the gift of prophecy in the local assembly.

- Prophetic ministry during an assembled church meeting should be by "two or three prophets and let the other judge" (1 Corinthians 14:29).

- Prophecies are to be given "one by one," that there be no confusion in the assembly or local church.

  "For ye may all prophesy one by one, that all may learn, and all may be comforted. And the spirits of the prophets are subject to the prophets. For God is not the author of confusion, but of peace, as in all churches of the saints" (1 Corinthians 14:31-33, Emphasis added).

- No prophecy should change the flow or order of a service. Nor should prophecy disrupt the service in any way. The Holy Spirit doesn't interfere with Himself. Scripture says, "Let all things be done decently and in order" (1 Corinthians 14:40).

APERCU

The simplest definition of a prophet is one who is a mouthpiece for God.

Prophecy is the Word of God spoken from the mouth of men.

Prophecy comes after a divine unction or urging from the Holy Spirit to prophesy.

All prophecy should be judged.

We should never be afraid of prophets because they utter God's good thoughts toward us.

The Holy Spirit will never violate, in word, deed, or spirit, the logos i.e., the Scriptures.

A true prophetic word has understandable meaning.

Scripture is clear. Even if a prophecy is presented with signs and wonders coming to pass, if it causes you to "go after other gods" it is not from the Lord.

One should have an inner witness "knowing" that the prophecy is accurate. "But you have an unction from the Holy One, and you know all things" (1 John 2:20).

Prophetic ministry during an assembled church meeting should be by "two or three prophets and let the other judge" (1 Corinthians 14:29).

Reflect & Apply

PROPHETS AND PROPHECY

1. Jesus gave _____, the Holy Spirit gave _____.

2. What prophet was called by God while tending his flocks?

_____

3. Name four ways that prophecy will come?

     1. _____

     2. _____

     3. _____

     4. _____

4. What did the Apostle Paul tell Timothy to stir up?

_____

5. What Scripture teaches us that prophets should never lose control over themselves?

_____

6. What are the three sources of all prophecy?

   1. _____

   2. _____

   3. _____

7. What should happen after hearing a prophecy?

_____

8. What does it mean to "try the spirits?"

_____

_____

_____

_____

_____

_____

_____

9. What should you do if your spirit man does not bear witness with a prophetic word? Explain.

_____

_____

_____

_____

_____

10. What is a conditional prophecy? Explain.

_____

_____

_____

_____

_____

NOTES

_____

_____

_____

_____

_____

_____

_____

_____

_____

_____

_____

_____

_____

PROPHECY: A VITAL MINISTRY

In this lesson we discover various ways for receiving prophetic revelation from the Lord.

We don't have to fear prophets or the prophetic voice of God because God's thoughts toward us are "thoughts of peace and not of evil to give you a future and a hope" (Jeremiah 29:11).

Prophecy is revealing the mind and will of God. It connects the spiritual realm to the natural realm. It is a supernatural communication of our Lord's will offering edification, exhortation, comfort, reassurance, warning and direction.

> Prophecy (rhema) is never used to replace or supersede the Bible (logos) and will never violate Scripture.

Prophetic communication today, often referred to as a word from the Lord, rhema, prophecy, or a "now" word from God, should never be placed on par with Scripture. In fact, all prophetic communication, no matter how spiritual sounding or exciting, should be submitted and judged according to the written Word of God, the logos. One of the sure signs of a true prophetic word from God is found in what that word produces in the life of the believer.

- True prophetic communication will always produce stability, balance, order, and a greater love for Jesus and His people.

VARIOUS WAYS OF COMMUNICATION

Prophets receive revelation and prophetic communication from God through various ways including:

1. Dreams – Joseph's prophetic dream (See Genesis 37:6-10). God warns the wise men to avoid King Herod. (See Matthew 2:12.)

2. Visions – Ezekiel's vision of the throne of God (See Ezekiel 1:1; 8:1-2); Isaiah saw Him high and lifted up (See Isaiah 6:1); Paul was caught up into the third heaven (See 2 Corinthians 12:2-4); and Zechariah had a vision of the man with a measuring line in his hand (See Zechariah 2:1). There are at least 17 others who are mentioned as having visions in the Word.

3. Angelic encounters – John before the throne (See Revelation 4.)

4. Prayer and intercessions

5. Words of knowledge and wisdom

6. Unction's (urgings and promptings) of the Holy Spirit

7. Trance – Peter had a trance. (See Acts 10:10; 11:15.) The Apostle Paul had a trance. (See Acts 22:17.)

IMPORTANT TO THE LOCAL CHURCH

Prophetic manifestations are a sign of the presence of the Holy Spirit. These manifestations also depict a healthy church. The prophetic ministry is very important to the local church in areas of:

- spiritual warfare (See 1 Timothy 1:18.)

- deliverance

- understanding times and seasons

- decrees and announcements (See Amos 3:7.)

- various levels of intercessions (See Chapter 6, The Watchman's Ministry.)

- depth of spiritual life

- encourages the weak (See 2 Chronicles 15:8.)

- prophetic strategies (See below.)

- warnings (See Acts 11:27-28; 20:22-23; 21:4,11.)

- impartation of gifts (See 1 Timothy 4:14.)

- setting apart for ministry (See Acts 13:14.)

- teaching (See 1 Corinthians 14:31.)

PROPHETIC STRATEGIES

As watchmen, prophets are called to "stand in the gap," and "make up the hedge." (See Ezekiel 22:30.)

They are anointed by our Lord to deliver and guard. (See Hosea 12:13.) They are given godly strategies that assist the local church in actively moving forward in the things of God. Prophetic strategies include:

- Elisha warned the king of Israel of the Syrian's intentions. "Elisha telleth the king of Israel the words that you speak in your bed chamber" (2 Kings 6:8-12).

- Naaman was healed of leprosy through prophetic instruction and strategy. "Wash in the Jordan seven times" (2 Kings 5:10-14).

- Elijah ministered to the widow woman in Zarephath. "Do as thou hast said but make me thereof a little cake first" (1 Kings 17:8-16).

All of the Scriptures above are examples of a unique prophetic communication coupled with strategies for receiving from the Lord.

- Prophets are skilled in understanding and crafting various spiritual weapons of warfare when faced with occult opposition against the local church.

- Said to be "second" (1 Corinthians 12:28), prophets are included as foundational ascension gifts and vital to building strong spiritual strength in the life of the local church.

Prophets are often misunderstood because of the prophetic grace on their lives, but with knowledge of their operations the Church can benefit from their unique and important ministry.

ROLE OF THE PROPHET IN THE LOCAL ASSEMBLY

1. Prophets should be submitted to the set man (leader) of the local church. (See Romans 13:1-4.)

2. Prophets should carry and advance the vision that the set man has introduced to the local church.

3. Prophets should guard the local church and leadership from demonic assignments such as: Jezebel spirits, witchcraft, divination, sin, false associations and demonic devices.

4. Prophets should deal with spiritual climates through prayer and intercessions, changing from hard to those more conducive to a move of God.

5. Prophets should transfer a desire to pray to the congregation.

6. Prophets should impart a love for God's prophetic voice.

7. Prophets should help in matters of deliverance and spiritual warfare.

APERCU

Prophets receive revelation and prophetic communication from God through various ways.

Prophetic presence is a sign of a healthy church.

As watchmen, prophets are called to "stand in the gap," and "make up the hedge." (See Ezekiel 22:30.)

Prophets are skilled in understanding and crafting various spiritual weapons of war when faced with occult opposition against the local church.

Said to be "second" (1 Corinthians 12:28), prophets are included as foundational in nature and vital to building strong spiritual strength in the life of the local church.

Reflect & Apply

PROPHECY A VITAL MINISTRY

1. Prophetic words should never be placed on par with _____.

2. Name three of the various ways prophets receive communication from God.

    1. _____

    2. _____

    3. _____

3. What are prophetic manifestations a sign of?

_____

_____

4. Prophets are called to _____ and make up the _____.

5. Who was healed through a prophetic strategy by Elijah?

_____

6. Who received a prophetic strategy that helped fight the Syrian army?

_____

_____

7. Who should prophets be submitted to in the local church? Explain why.

_____

_____

_____

_____

8. What desire should prophets transfer to a local congregation?

_____

_____

9. What love should prophets impart to a local congregation?

_____

_____

10. Name three things prophets should guard the local church from.

    1. _____

    2. _____

    3. _____

NOTES

THE WATCHMAN'S MINISTRY

God's prophetic sentinels are vital to the Church. In this lesson we learn about the ministry of the watchman.

Being a prophetic spokesman for the Lord is not the only ministry of a prophet; prophets are also watchmen who report what they see and hear.

SENTINELS

Ancient cities provided places of refuge and safety for their citizens. Massive walls fortified these cities. Faithful sentinels manned watchtowers to guard the city at night. When the gates were closed the city was secure from bandits and invaders. Many of these watchmen would spend days and nights without end, never seeing anything worth reporting. Faithful sentinels, however, never abandoned their post. They continued to keep watch over the city.

One can only imagine the great responsibility of such service to the city's residents. We can liken the prophet's ministry to the ancient sentinels who stood guard over their cities.

- A watchman is one called to stand guard, to keep watch, and say what he sees.

> "<u>I have set watchmen upon thy walls</u>, O Jerusalem, which shall never hold their peace day nor night: ye that make mention of the LORD, keep not silence…" (Isaiah 62:6, Emphasis added).

> "For thus hath the Lord said unto me, Go, set a watchman, let him declare what he seeth" (Isaiah 21:6).

The word "watchman" comes from the Hebrew word *shamar* with various meanings throughout Scripture, including:

- to keep

- observe

- heed

- preserve

- beware

- mark

- watchman

- wait

- watch

- regard

- preserve

- save.

GAPS AND HEDGES

God has placed prophetic ministry in gaps and hedges.

> "And I sought for a man among them that should make up the hedge, and stand in the gap before me for the land, that I should not destroy it: but I found none" (Ezekiel 22:30).

> "Standing in the gap" and "making up the hedge" are two of the primary ministries of the prophet.

Prophets stand in the gap through watching, prayer and intercession.

> "And he saw that there was no man, and wondered that there was no intercessor: therefore his arm brought salvation unto him; and his righteousness, it sustained him" (Isaiah 59:16, Emphasis added).

Prophets, as watchmen, are called to:

- watch

- identify

- warn

- signal

- provide security

- stand in towers (high places with good visibility).

A prophetic guard is likened to a sentinel who is assigned to protect or oversee the welfare of another.

PROPHETS AS PROTECTORS

Scripture says, "By a prophet the Lord brought Israel out of Egypt and by a prophet was he preserved" (Hosea 12:13). The word "preserved" comes from the Hebrew word *shamar*, meaning:

- guard

- keep

- watch

- save

- protect.

WARNINGS

The prophet's ministry is also called to warn of looming danger.

Scripture declares, "You will hear a message (word) from my mouth, and give them warning from me" (Ezekiel 33:7).

> "Son of man, I have made thee a watchman unto the house of Israel: therefore hear the word at my mouth, and give them warning from me" (Ezekiel 3:17).

GREAT RESPONSIBILITY

Watching carries a great responsibility with it, not only for those that hear the word, but to the hearers themselves.

> "But if the watchman see the sword come, and blow not the trumpet, and the people be not warned; if the sword come, and take any person from among them, he is taken away in his iniquity; but his blood will I require at the watchman's hand" (Ezekiel 33:6, Emphasis added).

> "When I say unto the wicked, Thou shalt surely die; and thou givest him not warning, nor speakest to warn the wicked from his wicked way, to save his life; the same wicked man shall die in his iniquity; but his blood will I require at thine hand. Yet if thou warn the wicked and he turn not from his wickedness, nor from his wicked way, he shall die in his iniquity; but thou hast delivered thy soul" (Ezekiel 3:18-19, Emphasis added).

WATCHMEN REPORT

- Watchmen are called to report information to those in authority.
  (See 2 Samuel 18:24.)

- Watchmen discern the difference between friend and foe.
  (See 2 Kings 9:17-20.)

PROPHETIC ASSURANCE

Not only will the prophet warn of impending danger, he will also comfort and encourage when one is moving in the right direction.

Prophets deal with:

- hope

- purpose

- life issues

- warnings

- guidance.

To guide means:

- to point the way

- direct on course

- give instruction

- provide insight.

WATCHMEN EXAMPLES

An example of a prophetic watchman in the Word:

- Agabus warning of a famine.

"And in these days came prophets from Jerusalem unto Antioch. And there stood up one of them named Agabus, and signified by the Spirit that there should be great dearth throughout all the world: which came to pass in the days of Claudius Caesar. Then the disciples, every man according to his ability, determined to send relief unto the brethren which dwelt in Judaea: Which also they did, and sent it to the elders by the hands of Barnabas and Saul" (Acts 11:27-30).

APERCU

Being a prophetic spokesman for the Lord is not the only ministry of a prophet; prophets are also watchmen who report what they see and hear.

A watchman is one called to stand guard, to keep watch, and to say what he sees.

The word "watchman" comes from the Hebrew word *shamar* with various meanings throughout Scripture, including to keep, observe, heed, preserve, beware, mark, watchman, wait, watch, regard, preserve, and save.

"Standing in the gap" and "making up the hedge" are two of the primary ministries of the prophet.

A prophetic guard is likened to a sentinel who is assigned to protect or oversee the welfare of another.

The word "preserved" comes from the Hebrew word *shamar*, meaning, guard, keep, watch, save, and protect.

The prophet's ministry is also called to warn of looming danger.

Watching carries with it a great responsibility.

Watchmen are called to report information to those in authority. (See 2 Samuel 18:24.)

Not only will the prophet warn of impending troubles, he will also comfort and encourage when one is moving in the right direction.

NOTES

_____

_____

_____

_____

_____

_____

_____

_____

_____

Reflect & Apply

THE WATCHMAN'S MINISTRY

1. What was the responsibility of ancient sentinels?

_____

_____

_____

_____

2. What is a watchman called to do? Explain.

_____

_____

_____

_____

3. What does the Hebrew word *shamar* mean? _____

4. How do prophets "stand in the gap"?

_____

_____

_____

_____

5. Who do the watchmen report to in the local church?

_____

_____

_____

6. How did the prophet Agabus demonstrate the ministry of a watchman? (Acts 11: 27-30) What was the outcome? Explain.

_____

_____

_____

_____

_____

_____

_____

_____

_____

_____

_____

_____

_____

_____

_____

_____

_____

NOTES

PROPHETIC COMMUNICATIONS

In this lesson we explore the unique ways God communicates with His prophets.

The dominant gift in the Old Testament was the prophet. There are several Hebrew words worth studying that will help us understand prophetic ministry along with various forms of prophetic communication. They are:

- Nabi

- Ra'ah

- Chozeh.

Let's review each of them.

NABI

The word *nabi* is first mentioned in relation to Abraham. Scripture says, "Now restore the man his wife; for he is a prophet (nabi) and he shall pray for thee, and thou shall live; and if thou restore her not, know thou that thou shalt surely die, thou and all that are thine" (Genesis 20:7).

The word nabi (prophet) is generally understood as one who is a spokesman for God, but more specifically is a form of prophetic communication through hearing the word of the Lord in one's spirit. This form of prophetic communication comes primarily by "the word of the Lord" rather than dreams and visions. There are many examples of nabi prophetic communication in the word of God. In fact, "The word of the Lord came unto me saying" is mentioned 45 times in Jeremiah, Ezekiel and Zechariah. Examples include:

- "Then the word of the LORD came unto me, saying" (Jeremiah 1:4).

- "Moreover the word of the LORD came unto me, saying, Jeremiah, what seest thou? And I said, I see a rod of an almond tree" (Jeremiah 1:11).

- "Then the word of the LORD came unto me, saying" (Jeremiah 13:8).

- "Again the word of the LORD came unto me, saying" (Jeremiah 24:4).

- "And Jeremiah said, the word of the LORD came unto me, saying" (Jeremiah 32:6).

The prophet Samuel began his ministry receiving prophetic communication on the nabi level but later progressed into a ra'ah (seer) prophet. The word nabi (prophet) is used in Old Testament Scripture in 316 verses.

- "Now the acts of David the king, first and last, behold, they are written in the book of Samuel the seer, and in the book of Nathan the prophet, and in the book of Gad the seer" (1 Chronicles 29:29).

- "And all Israel from Dan even to Beersheba knew that Samuel was established to be a prophet (ra-ah, seer) of the LORD" (1 Samuel 3:20).

RA'AH

The ra'ah prophet is the seer.

- The ra' ah form of prophetic communication receives revelation through dreams, visions, angels or visual prophetic symbolism.

- Samuel was referred to as a ra'ah prophet. "Come let us go to the seer" (ra'ah). (See 1 Samuel 9:19, 27.)

- Many times in Scripture we see God asking the prophets, "What seest thou?" (See Jeremiah 1:11, 13; 24:3; Amos 7:8; 8:2; Zechariah 4:2; 5:2.)

- The ra'ah prophet sees and hears when one comes before him. (See Ezekiel 14:4-7.) The type of things this prophet sees are not through natural seeing or hearing abilities but are visible and audible only in the spiritual realm.

- Elijah could see into the bedchamber of his enemy. (See 2 Kings 6:11.)

- Habakkuk declared, "I will watch to see" (Habakkuk 2:1).

CHOZAH

Our next prophetic communication is discovered in the word *chozeh*.

- The Old Testament chozeh prophetic communication came through beholding visions.

- Chozeh, open visions, are the highest level of prophetic communication.

- Ezekiel said, "The heavens were opened and I saw visions of God and I looked" (Ezekiel 1:1-4).

All of these are various means the Holy Spirit uses for prophet communication. Having the knowledge of these various words will give you an understanding of where you are at in your prophetic development.

Can you find other examples of this level of open visions in the Bible? Name one and include a Scriptural reference:_____

_____

_____

_____

_____

_____

APERCU

The dominant gift in the Old Testament was the prophet.

The word *nabi* is generally understood as one who is a spokesman for God, but more specifically is a form of prophetic communication through hearing the word of the Lord in one's spirit.

The ra'ah prophet sees and hears when one comes before him. (See Ezekiel 14:4-7.)

The ra'ah form of prophetic communication receives revelation through dreams, visions, angels or visual prophetic symbolism.

Chozeh, open visions, are the highest level of prophetic communication.

NOTES

_____
_____
_____
_____
_____
_____
_____
_____
_____
_____
_____
_____
_____

Reflect & Apply

PROPHETIC COMMUNICATIONS

1. What was the dominant gift in the Old Testament?

_____

_____

2. Name the three Hebrew words that help us understand prophetic communication.

    1. _____

    2. _____

    3. _____

3. Who was the first person to be referred to as a nabi?

_____

_____

4. Nabi prophetic communication comes primarily in what manner?

_____

_____

5. What statement is repeated many times in Jeremiah, Ezekiel and Zechariah?

_____

_____

6. A ra'ah prophet is a _____.

7. The ra'ah form of prophetic communication is received in what manner?

_____

_____

_____

_____

8. By what name was the Prophet Samuel referred?

_____

_____

9. How did the chozeh prophetic communication come to a prophet?

_____

_____

10. What is the highest level of prophetic communication?

_____

_____

_____

_____

_____

_____

ANNOUNCE, CONFIRM, ACTIVATE

One of the most interesting ministries of the prophet is found in prophetic announcements. In this lesson we will learn how God uses prophetic decrees to launch new events in the lives of believers.

We have discovered that the scope of the prophetic ministry is larger than most realize. In fact, nothing new will happen without a prophetic announcement coming first.

- To announce means to make known by formal notice.

- Prophetic announcements are the foretelling (predictive) operations through prophetic ministry of things to come.

- Prophetic announcements reveal the mind and will of the Lord regarding people and nations.

⚿ Scripture declares, "Surely the Lord GOD will do nothing, but he revealeth his secret unto his servants the prophets" (Amos 3:7).

- "The secret things belong unto the LORD our God: but those things which are revealed belong unto us and to our children for ever, that we may do all the words of this law" (Deuteronomy 29:29). (Notice the use of the word "revealed" to indicate what belongs to the believer.)

PROPHETIC ANNOUNCEMENTS

Prophets deal with times and seasons by announcing the end and the beginning of things. The following are seven examples of prophetic announcements that unlocked times and seasons in another's life. We, too, can expect to have spiritual seasons prophetically announced and unlocked to us. Notice in the following examples that nothing happened until a prophetic announcement took place.

1. Angel of the Lord to Mary (Luke 1:28-33)

One of the most well known prophetic announcements was to Mary, the mother of Jesus. The angel of the Lord told her that she was highly favored and would bring forth a son named Jesus who would be the Savior of the world. This announcement changed Mary's life forever. It opened the door for a new season in her life.

2. John the Baptist of the Lord (John 1:29)

John the Baptist made a prophetic announcement when he declared, "Behold the Lamb of God, which taketh away the sin of the world." John the Baptist was the forerunner of Christ's ministry. From this we learn that even in Jesus' ministry there was a prophetic announcement. This prophetic announcement revealed a new season in our Lord's ministry.

3. Samuel to David (1 Samuel 16)

Samuel made a prophetic announcement and impartation when he took a horn of oil and anointed David in the midst of his brethren. When he did this the Spirit of the Lord came upon David from that day forward. God unlocked a new season in his life through a prophetic operation.

4. The Angel to Gideon (Judges 6:12)

The angel of the Lord made a prophetic announcement to Gideon when he said, "Go in this thy might, and thou shalt save Israel from the hand of the Midianites: have not I sent thee?" Prior to this prophetic release Gideon had seen himself as the least in his father's house. This announcement stirred faith and action for a new day in Gideon's heart. The prophetic proclamation unlocked a new season in Gideon's life.

5. God to Moses (Exodus 4)

One day Moses climbed the mountain to see the great sight of the burning bush. The Lord spoke to him and told him that he had heard the cry of the children of Israel because of their great oppression. Then God prophetically announced to Moses his ministry of deliverance, "Come now therefore, and I will send thee unto Pharaoh, that thou mayest bring forth my people the children of Israel out of Egypt" (Exodus 4:10). Moses was impacted mightily by this prophetic decree. A new season was unlocked to him.

6. Joseph's Prophetic Dream (Genesis 37:6-10)

Joseph received a prophetic dream that announced a coming dominion authority. This prophetic dream so angered his brothers that they sought means to kill him and sold him into slavery.

7. Paul & Barnabas (Acts 13:3)

The Antioch church's presbytery made a prophetic announcement by the unction of the Holy Spirit as they were ministering to the Lord and fasting: "Separate me Barnabas and Saul for the work whereunto I have called them." Then they laid their hands on them and sent them (*apo-stello*) away. The prophetic announcement in the church at Antioch opened the door for a new season in Barnabas and Saul's ministry.

CONFIRMATION, IMPARTATION AND ACTIVATION

Not only does the prophetic gift deliver prophetic announcements of the will of God, it also provides confirmation, impartation and activation. See if you can identify what is happening in each representation in the following examples.

- Moses & Joshua (Deuteronomy 34:9)

Moses transferred the spirit of wisdom (grace on his life) to Joshua when he laid his hands on him. This prophetic impartation activated Joshua in a greater spiritual capacity.

- Timothy & Presbytery (1 Timothy 4:14)

Timothy received the Holy Spirit and activation in ministry through a prophetic presbytery.

- Saul & Ananias (Acts 9:17)

Saul (Apostle Paul) received an impartation and activation into ministry when the prophet Ananias laid his hands on him. It was through the prophetic ministry of Ananias that we learn of Paul being confirmed and activated into ministry.

- Elijah & Elisha (2 Kings 2:13)

When Elijah was taken up into heaven he threw down his mantel and Elisha grabbed it and struck the waters with it. The other prophets acknowledged that the spirit of Elijah then rested on Elisha and they came to meet him and bowed themselves to the ground before him. Elisha's ministry was confirmed, activated and a new season was unlocked to him.

APERCU

Prophetic announcements reveal the mind and will of the Lord regarding people and nations.

To announce means to make known by formal notice.

One of the most well known prophetic announcements was to Mary, mother of Jesus. The angel of the Lord told her that she was highly favored and would bring forth a son named Jesus who would be the Savior of the world.

Even in Jesus' ministry there was a prophetic announcement.

Samuel made a prophetic announcement and impartation when he took a horn of oil and anointed David in the midst of his brethren.

A prophetic proclamation unlocked a new season in Gideon's life.

Moses was impacted mightily by a prophetic decree. A new season had been unlocked to him.

Joseph received a prophetic dream that announced a coming dominion authority in his life.

The prophetic announcement in the church at Antioch opened the door for a new season in Barnabas and Saul's ministry.

Not only does the prophetic gift deliver prophetic announcements of the will of God it also provides confirmation, and activation.

Timothy received the Holy Spirit and activation in ministry through a presbytery.

It was through the prophetic ministry of Ananias that we learn of Paul being confirmed and activated into ministry.

When Elijah was taken up into heaven he threw down his mantel and Elisha grabbed it and struck the waters with it.

NOTES

_____

_____

_____

_____

_____

_____

_____

_____

_____

Reflect & Apply

ANNOUNCE, CONFIRM, ACTIVATE

1. What do prophetic announcements reveal?

_____

_____

_____

2. What was the prophetic announcement to Mary?

_____

_____

3. What was the prophetic announcement in Jesus' ministry?

_____

_____

4. Who made the prophetic announcement that David would be king?

_____

5. What was revealed to Joseph in a prophetic dream?

_____

_____

6. What prophetic announcement was made in the Antioch church? (Acts 13)

_____

_____

7. How did Moses impart the spirit of wisdom to Joshua?

_____

_____

_____

8. How did Timothy receive activation in ministry?

_____

_____

9. What happened when the Prophet Ananias prayed for Saul?

_____

_____

10. To announce means to _____

_____.

NOTES

EXTENSIVE TRAINING PROCESS

God puts all His prophets through intensive training. In this lesson we study prophetic protocol and conduct.

As one sets his or her desire to enter the prophetic ministry by responding to His divine grace, they must first enter God's extensive training process. (See 2 Peter 1:3-10.)

Every prophet will be thoroughly trained by the Holy Spirit to either cultivate character or break undesirable characteristics, specifically in such areas as:

- Pride – an excessively high opinion of oneself; conceit; haughtiness; superiority lofty air; contempt of others; better than.

- Arrogance – an overbearing pride, exorbitant claims of rank; exalting one's importance to an undue degree.

- Independence – self-governing; self-reliant; loyal to no one.

- Morality – biblical standards of conduct.

- Holiness – freedom from the entanglements of sin.

- Keeping one's word – truthfulness; honesty and integrity.

- In giving of tithes and offerings – obedience to God's Word in giving is an indication of submission to being personally governed by His Word.

- Obedience – the act of obeying; compliance; words or actions denoting submission to authority.

- Commitment level – dedication to a longtime course of action.

- Relationships toward others – interrelating with others.

- Love for one another.

INDEPENDENT PROPHETS

There is no such thing as an independent prophet. True prophets understand that they can never be free from the influence, guidance, and input from others. Prophets must understand their calling and set place inside the local church.

- All five-fold ascension gifts are set "in" the local church. (See 1 Corinthians 12:27-28.)

The area of independence and submission is a dominant objective of the Holy Spirit.

One cannot go far in the prophetic that has an independent, "Rambo," free drifting, gotta do it my way, or rogue mentality.

Pride and arrogance often tempt the young prophet, who sometimes forgets he is only one spoke in God's Church wheel. A man once said, "One spoke on a wheel still arrives at the same destination."

PROPHETIC PROTOCOL AND PERSPECTIVE

When you enter the prophetic dimension the Holy Spirit will begin to change your orientation, pursuit and direction in ministry. Just as the date on a clock is reset or dials on instruments are reset, so does God reset the prophetic candidate's protocol and perspective of ministry.

> The English understanding of the word protocol is "a code of conduct."

Just as there is a code of conduct, or protocol, when serving as a diplomatic representative or ambassador of a nation, there is also a code of conduct for the prophet who is an ambassador of Christ. True prophets are a class act. Let's examine the word *protocol*. Protocol comes from two Greek words: "proto" and "col."

- The word *proto* is a Greek word meaning "to be first."

- *Col* comes from the Greek word *collum*, meaning "to be the original dispatch, instrument, deed, or that, which is seen or heard first."

- Therefore, prophetic protocol is a form of conduct by one who is called as a first dispatch.

PROPHETIC CONDUCT

Often, developing prophets discredit the protocol of the prophetic by not understanding the role of prophetic conduct. This is why God offers an extensive training process for his prophetic representatives. Prophets must learn how to…

- carry spiritual burdens (See Ezekiel 2:10.)

- understand when (timing) to release a prophetic word

- submit to spiritual and natural authority

- the role of prophets in society (the marketplace) and the local church

- the statesmanship as a prophetic representative of the Lord Jesus Christ.

RESETTING AND NEW DESIRES

As the prophet grows in the things of the Lord, the Holy Spirit will reset his or her protocols by changing the heart's desires. When you install new computer software into your computer, for example, you most often have to reboot your system. So you mouse over and restart the computer. The new software upgrades your system registry with the new files and your new software then integrates with your computer and runs properly.

Just like installing new software on your computer, when you begin to pursue the realm of the prophetic the Holy Spirit will reset you by changing your perspective and orientation of ministry. As He downloads a new perspective of ministry and a deeper level of spiritual sensitivity into your heart, what used to be important seems not to mean much anymore. In fact, you can sense that there has been an upgrade in your purpose as you pursue a more intimate walk with the Lord.

APERCU

All prophets enter an extensive training process.

There is no such thing as an independent prophet.

Prophets must understand their calling and set place inside the local church.

The English understanding of the word *protocol* is "a code of conduct."

The word *proto* is a Greek word meaning "to be first."

Col comes from the Greek word *collum*, meaning "to be the original dispatch, instrument, deed, or that, which is seen or heard first."

Prophetic protocol is a form of conduct by one who is called as a first dispatch.

NOTES

_____
_____
_____
_____
_____
_____
_____
_____
_____
_____

Reflect & Apply

EXTENSIVE TRAINING PROCESS

1. Prophets go through an _____.

2. What is the first thing a prophet must do after receiving a divine call?

_____

_____

3. What is arrogance?

_____

_____

_____

4. What is an independant prophet?

_____

_____

_____

5. What is the definition of morality?

_____

_____

_____

6. What does it mean for a prophet to be obedient?

_____

_____

7. There is no such thing as an _____ prophet.

8. What are two things that often tempt the young prophet?

    1. _____

    2. _____

9. What does God reset in the prophet's life?

_____

_____

_____

_____

10. What does the Greek word *proto* mean?

_____

_____

11. Define the Greek word *collum*.

_____

_____

12. What is prophetic protocol?

_____

Chapter 10

SUPERNATURAL EDUCATION

In this lesson our prophetic schooling takes us into spiritual warfare, deliverance and various types of prayers.

The Holy Spirit educates prophets in the spiritual and supernatural dimension, praise and worship, prayer, various levels of intercessions, spiritual warfare, deliverance, and character development.

- Deliverance ministry is a major facet of the prophetic dimension.

The ministry of the prophetic is one that deals with spiritual hindrances toward the advancement of the Gospel of Jesus Christ in territories and the building of strong governing churches. It identifies anything that hinders one's personal advancement in intimacy with the Lord Jesus Christ. Hence, the ministry of the prophet is more than a prediction center, but speaks into the very belief systems and inner core of every believer. The prophetic attacks and tears down strongholds in one's mind. (See 2 Corinthians 10:3-6.)

All prophets should be well versed in the following:

SPIRITUAL WARFARE

Spiritual warfare is a method of intercession that uses the authority of the believer to pray against spiritual forces of wickedness in heavenly places.

As deliverance prayer deals with hurts, wounds or demonic activity in people, spiritual warfare deals with principalities and powers in the heavens. (See Jeremiah 1:10; Ephesians 6:10-19.)

DELIVERANCE

One of the first things that Jesus did in His ministry was cast out a devil. Jesus never taught His apostles, or anyone else, to ignore the devil.

> "And Jesus rebuked him, saying, Hold thy peace, and come out of him. And when the devil had thrown him in the midst, he came out of him, and hurt him not. And they were all amazed, and spake among themselves, saying, what a word is this! For with authority and power he commandeth the unclean spirits, and they come out. And the fame of him went out into every place of the country round about" (Luke 35-37, Emphasis added).

Mrs. Jesse Penn-Lewis, in collaboration with the great Welsh Revivalist Evan Roberts, circa 1880, wrote of a satanic confederacy of wicked spirits and the importance of not ignoring them. She wrote,

> "A perspective view of the ages covered by the history in Bible records, shows that the rise and fall in spiritual power of the people of God was marked by the recognition of the existence of the demoniacal hosts of evil. When the

Church of God in the old and new dispensations was at the highest point of spiritual power, the leaders recognized, and drastically dealt with, the invisible forces of Satan; and when at the lowest they were ignored, or allowed to have free course among the people."

(*War on the Saints*, p. 27, 1909, Overcomer Book Room, Bournemouth, Hants, England.)

PRAYER AND INTERCESSION

Prophets are drawn into prayer and intercessions. There are many different kinds of prayer and intercessions. Such as:

1. Prayer that doesn't give up – importunity (Luke 18:6-8)

2. Prayer of faith (James 5:15; Matthew 21:22; Mark 11:24)

3. Deliverance prayer (Acts 16:18)

4. Binding and loosing (Matthew 16:19)

5. Prayer of agreement (Matthew 18:18-20)

6. Praying in the Spirit (Jude 20; 1 Corinthians 14:4, 14:14-15; Isaiah 28:11-12; Acts 10:46)

7. Fervent effective prayer (James 5:16; Romans 12:11; Colossians 4:12)

8. Prayer of consecration and dedication (Luke 22:42)

9. Prayer of commitment (1 Peter 5:7)

10. Prayer of worship (Luke 24:52-53; Acts 13:1-4)

11. Corporate prayer (Acts 4:23-31)

12. Prayer with groaning and travail (Romans 8:26; Isaiah 66:8; Galatians 4:19; Jeremiah 30:6).

The grace on the prophet's life will impact and challenge every believer to spend more time in prayer and developing an intimate relationship with Jesus Christ.

- Prophets have a heart for the sheep. (See 1 Corinthians 13:2.)

Like all the ascension gifts, prophets are required to have a heart for the sheep, knowing that Jesus is the Master Builder of the Church and that He shed His blood for all. As the prophet grows in ministry, so should his or her people skills and ability to deal with others. Contrary to religious perception, the prophet is more than a spiritual warrior, but is also used by the Holy Spirit to help every believer grow and mature in the things of God. The unique grace on the life of the prophet is imparted to every believer.

APERCU

Deliverance ministry is a major facet of the prophetic dimension.

The prophetic attacks and tears down strongholds in one's mind. (See 2 Corinthians 10:3-6.)

Spiritual warfare is a method of intercession that uses the authority of the believer to pray against spiritual forces of wickedness in heavenly places.

One of the first things that Jesus did in His ministry was cast out a devil. (See Luke 4:35.)

Like all the ascension gifts, prophets are required to have a heart for the sheep.

NOTES

_____

_____

_____

_____

_____

_____

_____

_____

_____

_____

_____

_____

Reflect & Apply

SUPERNATURAL EDUCATION

1. The ministry of the prophet is more than a _____ center.

2. What does the prophet tear down in the minds of believers?

_____

_____

3. Name three things prophets should be well versed in.

    1. _____

    2. _____

    3. _____

4. What is spiritual warfare?

_____

_____

_____

_____

5. What was one of the first things Jesus did in His ministry?

_____

_____

6. Jesus never taught His apostles to ignore the _____.

7. What did Jesse Penn-Lewis write about the existence of a demonic host?

_____

_____

8. What kind of prayer never gives up?

_____

9. Prophets have a heart for _____. (See 1 Corinthians 13:2.)

10. List six kinds of prayer with Scriptural references.

    1. _____

    2. _____

    3. _____

    4. _____

    5. _____

    6. _____

EDIFY, EXHORT & CURSE?

In this lesson we learn the role of New Testament prophets in pronouncing judgments and curses on sinners.

From Isaiah to Jeremiah to Elisha, Old Testament prophets commonly pronounced judgments and curses on nations and peoples. In fact, prophesying doom and gloom on nations and pronouncing judgments on individuals was seemingly part and parcel of the prophetic ministry before Jesus Christ, the Prophet, became a curse for us.

Thousands of years later, some New Testament prophets are still operating in this flow, but are all of them speaking on behalf of the Spirit of God? Or could some of them be prophesying out of hurts and wounds, pride or some sinister spirit?

PROPHETIC JUDGEMENTS

At the heart of the matter is a single, yet critical question: Is it biblical for modern day prophets to pronounce judgments and curses on people and cities today?

When studying this question, the most obvious Scriptural examples of prophetic judgments are:

1. When Ananias and Sapphira were judged after lying to the Holy Ghost. (See Acts 5:1-11.)

2. When the Apostle Paul pronounced judgment and temporary blindness came on the sorcerer at the isle unto Paphos. (See Acts 13:4-12.)

Yet, are these two examples typical of the operations of the prophetic ministry? Or could they be uncommon and only extraordinary events? Let's examine the spirit of this issue.

QUESTIONABLE PROPHECIES

Anyone who has moved in prophetic circles has surely heard some questionable prophecies.

- Take, for example, the prophet who announces, "Mr. Government Official better repent for not taking my advice or he will die in nine months."

- Then there's the prophet who exerts control over his congregation by proclaiming, "If you leave this church, then something bad will happen to you!"

- Let's not forget the prophet who declares, "The stock market will crash because idolatry and sin has brought the wrath of God Almighty."

All of these judgments and curses are prefaced with "Thus saith the Lord." But did God really say that? Or has carelessness, hidden sin, the spirit of Jezebel, or some other ungodly influence led some prophets to tap into spirits that are anything but holy?

- Prophetic judgments are nothing new to the prophetic restoration that began in the 1980s, but unfortunately many such ill-advised, ill-conceived and downright dishonest declarations have caused believers to doubt or discount this vital ministry.

Practically every year someone somewhere in the world prophesies that God will send fires and earthquakes to California and floods and hurricanes to Florida. The reasoning for such prophetic judgments and curses is typically sin or disobedience to God. But just because an earthquake shakes California, or a hurricane approaches the shores of Florida doesn't make a prophetic word accurate or a prophet credible.

California fires and Florida storms are usually annual events. Florida lies directly in the path of hurricanes (note: hurricane is a Caribbean Indian word for "evil spirit" and "big wind") and South Florida averages some 10 storms every year.

- To prophesy such things is like saying, "The Spirit of God shows me that the water will be wet," or, "The government will be charging you sales tax on your next purchase."

- That's not to say that God doesn't reveal such devastating events to a prophet. He has and probably will again. Rather, it's the spirit behind the announcement that is cause for concern.

Still, prophets arise frequently to pronounce such stormy judgments on South Florida, California and beyond. Foretelling hurricanes became an especially popular prophecy after Hurricane Andrew killed 11 people and caused $1 billion damage in South Florida in 1992.

Thank God, the region has not seen another hurricane of that magnitude hit the area despite periodic erroneous prophetic announcements. But what happens when someone prophesies a hurricane and coincidentally gets it right? Could that advance a prophet's status in the eyes of unlearned believers?

JUDGMENT FROM GOD?

Let's ask some hard questions about the use of prophetic judgments.

- Could the purpose of the storm be the judgment of God because of sin?

- Does judgment draw people closer to God?

- Are prophetic curses revealing the mind and will of the Lord in order to scare an individual into repentance? Is that the character of God?

- Is it Scriptural for a prophet to pronounce curses and judgments as the result of sin?

Each question seems to lead to two others like it. But, again, the answers are found in the Word of God.

CURSES AND JUDGMENTS

There are several Scriptures to indicate that New Testament ascension gift prophets are not called to speak prophetic curses or judgments on the world.

- First of all, the Word says that unbelievers are judged already, if they don't believe in the Son of God. (See John 3:18.) So does it make sense to pronounce another curse against them?

- Scripture also says, "For God sent not his Son into the world to condemn the world; but that the world through him might be saved" (John 3:17).

- The Bible tells us that we have the ministry of reconciliation and that, "God was in Christ, reconciling the world unto himself, not imputing their trespasses unto them" (2 Corinthians 5:19).

- The word "imputing" comes from the Greek word logizomai, meaning "to consider the facts and to take them into account when making a decision."

- Therefore, this Scripture makes it clear that God is not considering the fact of our sins in rendering a decision about His intent toward the world. His desire is to reconcile the world back to Himself through His Son Jesus Christ.

- Certainly, God give every rank sinner every possible opportunity to be born again.

- Does it make sense that God would offer up His Son on a cross for the sins of the world and then send a prophet to pronounce judgment, curses, even everlasting death in an eternal fire on the very people He died for?

- Are we in a time of grace or not?

- Yes, one day there will be a resurrection of the just and the unjust, one to everlasting life and the other to everlasting judgment (see Acts 24:15; 2 Peter 2:9) but is to curse, pronounce death, sickness, trouble, fires, hurricanes or pain on people and cities because of sin Scriptural?

BLESS AND CURSE NOT

I went to an area in Nicaragua devastated by an earthquake in 2000. Hundreds of homes were destroyed and several little children were killed. I remember praying for a sobbing woman who was kneeling on a pile of rubble that was once her home. She had lost her only child, a two-year-old daughter, to a falling block wall.

I was shocked to discover so many people saying that God had sent the earthquake as a judgment against them. No, they weren't prophesying it, but it was the same spirit in the message. The result was an intense hatred toward God. The question of crying families was, "How can I love Jesus after He has destroyed my home and killed my children?"

- Jesus didn't destroy those homes and children. Jesus said, "The thief comes only to steal, kill and destroy, but I have come that they might have life and that they might have it more abundantly" (John 10:10).

- Paul said, "Love your enemies. Bless and curse not" (Romans 12:14).

- Yes, "Life and death are in the power of the tongue" (Proverbs 18:21) yet even Balaam said, "Behold, I have received commandment to bless: and he hath blessed; and I cannot reverse it" (Numbers 23:20).

THE PROPHET'S HEART

The other side of the prophetic coin deals with the prophet's heart. Certainly we have seen legitimate prophets predict the fall of evil governments and individuals receive true rebukes of the Spirit. The balance is found in the maturity and purity of the prophet's heart.

- The Lord may indeed show a prophet that an individual is going to die in six months if he does not change his ways, but should the prophet pronounce it as a judgment?

- Or should the prophet stand in the gap, make up the hedge and intercede for the person in faith?

Such prophetic revelation should grieve a holy prophet and spur him to action to intercede in prayer as the Spirit leads.

PROPHETIC MOTIVATION

A part of pronouncing curses and judgments boils down to motives.

- Is the prophet truly speaking what saith the Lord, no matter what the Lord saith – for good or bad?

- Or is the prophet decreeing destruction out of pride, arrogance, or rejection?

- Is the prophet seeking to be admired, feared or revered?

- Is the prophet speaking forth curses to put on an air of superiority or to look powerful? What kind of prophet would take any pleasure in cursing someone to death when Jesus came to bring life?

- While the Spirit of God can do as He wishes, the prophet in and of himself does not have any authority to curse or judge.

REBELLIOUS PROPHETS

Rebellious prophets, tapping into spirits of divination, are not following the biblical pattern for the New Testament prophetic ministry of edification, exhortation and comfort. Even rebellious Old Testament prophets met with God's rebuke.

- It's important to distinguish that a mature prophet can err, but that same prophet will admit his mistake and learn from it. That's why all prophecy needs to be judged.

- Prophets who intentionally set out to manipulate,control,deceive or otherwise harm people through prophetic judgments or curses are out of order.

So, is it part of the New Testament prophet's ministry to pronounce curses and judgments? While the answers are undoubtedly in the Word and we certainly have some solid foundational guidelines, no one has uncovered all of the truth in this matter yet.

Perhaps, then, we should all agree that more sensitivity, prayer and careful examination of such prophecies are warranted. I am convinced that a love for Jesus and the people He died for will help bring balance to this issue.

APERCU

There are several Scriptures to indicate that New Testament ascension gift prophets are not called to speak prophetic curses or judgments on the world.

"For God sent not his Son into the world to condemn the world; but that the world through him might be saved" (John 3:17).

The Bible tells us that we have the ministry of reconciliation and that, "God was in Christ, reconciling the world unto himself, not imputing their trespasses unto them" (2 Corinthians 5:19).

The word "imputing" comes from the Greek word logizomai, meaning to consider the facts and to take them into account when making a decision.

Certainly, God gives every rank sinner every possible opportunity to be born again.

Paul said, "Love your enemies. Bless and curse not" (Romans 12:14).

Yes, "Life and death are in the power of the tongue" (see Proverbs 18:21) yet even Balaam said, "Behold, I have received commandment to bless: and he hath blessed; and I cannot reverse it" (See Numbers 23:20).

A part of pronouncing curses and judgments boils down to motives.

Rebellious prophets, tapping into spirits of divination, are not following the biblical pattern for the New Testament prophetic ministry of edification, exhortation and comfort.

Reflect & Apply

EDIFY, EXHORT & CURSE?

1. What are the two most common reasons why some falsely prophesy judgements?

_____

_____

2. What are the most common judgment prophecies spoken about Florida and California?

     Florida:_____

     California: _____

3. If a prophecy of judgment was correct does that validate the prophet or the prophetic word? Explain.

_____

_____

_____

_____

4. Does judgment draw people closer to God?

_____

_____

5. Is it Scriptural for a prophet to pronounce curses and judgments as the result of sin?

_____

6. According to John 3:18, an unbeliever is already _____.

7. Describe the ministry of reconcilation.

_____

_____

_____

_____

8. What does the word imputing (*logizomai*) mean?

_____

_____

9. What does Scripture say regarding our enemies?

_____

10. What is the biblical pattern for New Testament prophetic ministry?

_____

_____

_____

EARMARKS OF FALSE PROPHETS

In this lesson we study the nature of false prophets.

Scripture says many false prophets have gone into the world, "Beloved, believe not every spirit, but try the spirits whether they are of God: because many false prophets are gone out into the world" (1 John 4:1).

Just as in the days of the Prophet Jeremiah false prophets abound today. They seldom address sin, rather they concentrate on accumulating wealth and power. False propehts do little or nothing to turn people from sin toward God.

The term "false prophet" cannot be found in the Old Testament; however, Jeremiah said that some prophets, "prophesy falsely." (See Jeremiah 5:31.) He also had much to say about unholy prophets who consistently hindered his ministry. Many Scriptural references can be found in Jeremiah Chapters 23 and 29.

The term "false prophet" does appear in the New Testament 11 times (Matthew 7:15; 24:11, 24; Mark 13:22; Luke 6:26; 2 Peter 2:1; 1 John 4:1; Acts 13:6; Revelation 16:13, 19:20, 20:10).

In this lesson let's look at some of the earmarks of a false prophet.

DECEITFUL

Deceit is the deliberate act or practice of deceiving, misleading, tricking or defrauding.

False prophets are deceitful workers. The word "deceive" comes from the Greek word *planao*, meaning to:

- cause to stray

- lead astray

- lead aside from the right way

- lead away from the truth

- lead into error

- sever from the truth.

"Many false prophets shall rise, and shall deceive many" (Matthew 24:11).

False prophets will also deceive their own selves. (See Jeremiah 14:13-16.)

MERCHANDISERS

One of the most common earmarks of a false prophet is their love of money, and their ways of merchandising God's people and falsely marketing themselves.

"But there were false prophets also among the people, even as there shall be false teachers among you, who privily shall bring in damnable heresies, even denying the Lord that bought them, and bring upon themselves swift destruction. And many shall follow their pernicious ways; by reason of whom the way of truth shall be evil spoken of. <u>And through covetousness shall they with feigned words make merchandise of you</u>: whose judgment now of a long time lingereth not, and their damnation slumbereth not" (2 Peter 2:1-3, Emphasis added).

False prophets love money and will sell the Gospel, the anointing and whatever else they can peddle for a buck. Beware the prophet that sells prophecy, healing, or anything else. Remember the words of the Apostle Peter, "Silver and gold have I none; but such as I have give I thee: In the name of Jesus Christ of Nazareth rise up and walk" (Acts 3:6).

Other Scriptures of merchandising prophets include:

- False prophets who divine for money (See Micah 3:11.)

- Love the wages of unrighteousness (See 2 Peter 2:15.)

- Greedy and for gainsaying (money) they perish (See Jude 11.)

MAY DEMONSTRATE GREAT SIGNS AND WONDERS

False prophets may even demonstrate powerful signs, wonders and miracles. But great signs and wonders do not validate a prophetic ministry.

"For there shall arise false Christs, and false prophets, and shall show great signs and wonders; insomuch that, if it were possible, they shall deceive the very elect" (Matthew 24:24).

Scripture declares that false prophets can display signs and wonders. We must never authenticate one's ministry by signs and wonders but rather what is said. Are they Scripturally sound in doctrine? This is the true test. Jesus said that you could know a tree by its fruit. What does it produce?

> "Even so every good tree bringeth forth good fruit; but a corrupt tree bringeth forth evil fruit. A good tree cannot bring forth evil fruit, neither can a corrupt tree bring forth good fruit. Every tree that bringeth not forth good fruit is hewn down, and cast into the fire. Wherefore by their fruits ye shall know them. Not every one that saith unto me, Lord, Lord, shall enter into the kingdom of heaven; but he that doeth the will of my Father which is in heaven. Many will say to me in that day, Lord, Lord, have we not prophesied in thy name? and in thy name have cast out devils? and in thy name done many wonderful works? And then will I profess unto them, I never knew you: depart from me, ye that work iniquity" (Matthew 7:17-23).

SEDUCERS

False prophets will seduce their victims. To seduce means to lure, entice, tempt, or beguile, in an effort to mislead.

> "For false Christs and false prophets shall rise, and shall show signs and wonders, to <u>seduce</u>, if it were possible, even the elect" (Mark 13:22, Emphasis added).

This word "seduce" comes from the Greek word *apoplanao*, which is from two Greek words "apo" and "planao." This speaks of a seduction that must occur first to lead one out or away from (*apo*) truth and into deception and error.

DISSENSION AND DIVISION

"But there were false prophets also among the people, even as there shall be false teachers among you, who privily shall bring in <u>damnable heresies</u>, even denying the Lord that bought them, and bring upon themselves swift destruction" (2 Peter 2:1, Emphasis added).

The word "heresies" comes from the Greek word *hairesis*, meaning "to cause dissension and division by a sect of false prophets who lead people astray through the introduction of a diversity of opinions."

SPEAK CURSES AND JUDGMENTS AGAINST GOD'S PEOPLE

Balaam was hired by King Balak to curse the people of God. He wanted the rewards for divination. (See Numbers 22:6-7.)

RAVENING WOLVES

"Beware of false prophets, which come to you in sheep's clothing, but inwardly they are ravening wolves" (Matthew 7:15).

ADULTEROUS

An adulterous prophet is one who is unfaithful and willing to break covenants and agreements.

"I have seen also in the prophets of Jerusalem a horrible thing: <u>they commit adultery</u>, and walk in lies: they strengthen also the hands of evildoers, that none doth return from his wickedness: they are all of them unto me as Sodom, and the inhabitants thereof as Gomorrah" (Jeremiah 23:14, Emphasis added).

CORRUPT

A corrupt prophet is morally polluted with tainted character, motivations and desires.

"For both prophet and priest are profane; yea, in my house have I found their wickedness, saith the LORD" (Jeremiah 23:11).

DRUNKEN

False prophets are given to drinking.

"But they also have erred through wine, and through strong drink are out of the way; the priest and the prophet have erred through strong drink, they are swallowed up of wine, they are out of the way through strong drink; they err in vision, they stumble in judgment" (Isaiah 28:7, Emphasis added).

PROPHESY FALSELY
(Jeremiah 6:13-14; 8:10-11; 23:13-14, 32; 29:23; Ezekiel 13:2, 17)

False prophets will speak without having received a prophetic word from God. (See Jeremiah 14:15; 23:21; 29:31.)

False prophets will prophesy with smooth, flattering sayings. (See Isaiah 30:10; Jeremiah 5:30-31; Amos 2:12.)

FOOLISH

Foolish prophets waste time prophesying meaningless things. (See Jeremiah 2:8; 29:23; Hosea 9:7.)

No one ever needs to prophesy the obvious like; the water is wet, etc.

False prophets prophesy things that, after a careful examination of the prophetic word, don't really mean anything. One prophet, for example, was heard saying that God told him the start and end date of the war in Iraq. The question was, "Why would God tell him that?" What difference did it make to know the start and end date of that war? The whole country knew that we were going to have a war breakout any day between the United States and Iraq. Could it be that prophecy like that is only used to make the prophet look more spiritual and connected to God than others?

Or one may prophesy a great change is going to take place in the United States in the next 90 days. Prophecy like that is nonsense. Of course, some where in the United States there is going to be some kind of a change take place.

GREEDY

(See Jeremiah 8:10; Micah 3:11; 2 Peter 2:3, 15.)

Greed is an excessive or insatiable desire to acquire or possess more than what one needs or deserves, especially with respect to material wealth.

"For from the least of them even unto the greatest of them every one is given to covetousness; and from the prophet even unto the priest every one dealeth falsely" (Jeremiah 6:13).

LYING

(See Jeremiah 6:13-14; 27:9, 10, 14, 18; Isaiah 9:14-16.)

False prophets will lie. A lie is a false statement deliberately presented as being true; a falsehood, something meant to deceive, or give a wrong impression.

> "And her prophets have daubed them with untempered mortar, seeing vanity, and <u>divining lies</u> unto them, saying, Thus saith the Lord GOD, when the LORD hath not spoken" (Ezekiel 22:28, Emphasis added).

MURDEROUS (shed blood)

Today, the false prophet will murder the reputation of others through slander and false accusations.

> "For the sins of her prophets, and the iniquities of her priests, that have <u>shed the blood of the just</u> in the midst of her. They have wandered as blind men in the streets, they have polluted themselves with blood, so that men could not touch their garments" (Lamentations 4:13-14, Emphasis added).

PRESUMPTUOUS

A presumptuous prophet goes beyond what is right or proper in the scope of prophetic ministry.

> A presumptuous prophet thinks that God wants to prophesy when He doesn't.

> A presumptuous prophet will prophesy without having received a word from God. (See Jeremiah 14:15; 23:21; 29:31.)

PROFANE (impure or defiled)

False prophets are impure and defile themselves and their prophecies.

> "<u>Her prophets are light and treacherous persons</u>: her priests have <u>polluted the sanctuary</u>, they have done violence to the law" (Jeremiah 23:14, Emphasis added).

> "I have seen also in the prophets of Jerusalem an horrible thing: they commit adultery, and walk in lies: they strengthen also the hands of evildoers, that none doth return from his wickedness: they are all of them unto me as Sodom, and the inhabitants thereof as Gomorrah" (Jeremiah 23:14).

RECKLESS AND IRRESPONSIBLE

A reckless prophet is indifferent to others and has an irresponsible disregard for the consequences of their actions.

> "Behold, I am against them that prophesy false dreams, saith the LORD, and do tell them, and <u>cause my people to err by their lies</u>, and by their lightness; yet I sent them not, nor commanded them: therefore they shall not profit this people at all, saith the LORD" (Jeremiah 23:32, Emphasis added).

THIEVING

False prophets steal popular prophetic buzzwords and sayings from other prophets. They are master mimics and imitators.

"Therefore, behold, I am against the prophets, saith the LORD, that <u>steal my words</u> every one from his neighbor" (Jeremiah 23:30, Emphasis added).

TREACHEROUS

False prophets are treacherous. One who is treacherous is marked by betrayal and cannot be trusted or relied upon.

"The watchman of Ephraim was with my God: but <u>the prophet is a snare of a fowler in all his ways</u>, and hatred in the house of his God" (Hosea 9:8, Emphasis added).

"Her prophets are light and <u>treacherous</u> persons: her priests have polluted the sanctuary, they have done violence to the law" (Zephaniah 3:4, Emphasis added).

SMOOTH FLATTERING PROPHECIES

False prophets will use flattering prophecies to gain acceptance and trust.

"Which say to the seers, See not; and to the prophets, prophesy not unto us right things, speak unto us smooth things, prophesy deceits" (Isaiah 30:10).

"A wonderful and horrible thing is committed in the land; the prophets <u>prophesy falsely</u>, and the priests bear rule by their means; and <u>my people love to have it so</u>: and what will ye do in the end thereof?" (Jeremiah 5:30-31, Emphasis added).

APERCU

Just as in the days of the Prophet Jeremiah false prophets abound today. They seldom address sin, rather they concentrate on accumulating wealth, power and do little or nothing to turn people from sin toward God.

Deceit is the deliberate act or practice of deceiving, misleading, tricking, or defrauding.

One of the most common earmarks of a false prophet is their love for money, and their ways of merchandising God's people and falsely marketing themselves.

Great signs and wonders do not validate a prophetic ministry.

To seduce means to lure, entice, tempt, or beguile, in an effort to mislead.

An adulterous prophet is one who is unfaithful and willing to break covenants and agreements.

A corrupt prophet is morally polluted with tainted character, motivations and desires.

Greed is an excessive or insatiable desire to acquire or possess more than what one needs or deserves, especially with respect to material wealth.

A lie is a false statement deliberately presented as being true; a falsehood, something meant to deceive, or give a wrong impression.

A presumptuous prophet goes beyond what is right or proper in the scope of prophetic ministry.

A reckless prophet is indifferent to others and has an irresponsible disregard for the consequences of their actions.

One who is treacherous is marked by betrayal and cannot be trusted or relied upon.

False prophets will use flattering prophecies to gain acceptance and trust.

NOTES

_____

_____

_____

_____

_____

_____

_____

_____

_____

_____

_____

_____

_____

_____

_____

_____

_____

_____

Reflect & Apply

EARMARKS OF FALSE PROPHETS

1. What does it mean to deceive? Explain.

_____

_____

_____

_____

2. What is the most common earmark of a false prophet?

_____

_____

3. Do signs and wonders validate a prophet? Explain.

_____

_____

_____

_____

4. How did Jesus teach us to know a person? Explain.

_____

_____

_____

5. Why was Balaam hired by King Balak?

_____

_____

6. False prophets will come to you dressed in what kind of clothing?

_____

7. Describe what greed is.

_____

_____

_____

8. What is a lie?

_____

_____

9. A presumptuous prophet will prophesy without _____

_____.

10. Describe a reckless prophet.

_____

_____

_____

11. What kind of prophecies will false prophets use to gain acceptance and trust?

_____

12. False prophets will steal the current prophet buzzwords and sayings from other _____

_____

NOTES

_____

_____

_____

_____

_____

_____

_____

_____

_____

_____

_____

_____

_____

_____

_____

_____

_____

_____

_____

_____

_____

_____

_____

_____

HALLMARKS OF THE PROPHET

In this study we learn the main traits of God's prophetic messengers.

THE SEER

The Old Testament prophet was called "a man of God" (see 1 Kings 12:22; 13:1, 26) "man of the spirit" (see Hosea 9:7 NCV), "God's servants" (see Jeremiah 7:25; 44:4) and "God's messengers" (See Haggai 1:13; Malachi 3:1).

In Israel the term "seer" was the title given a prophet. (See 1 Samuel 9:9.)

This seeing ability of a prophet is like being enabled by the Holy Spirit to draw back a curtain and see what is hidden behind it. One prophet said that being able to see spiritually was like pulling himself up on top of a wall and then looking on the other side. Of course, this can only be done as the Holy Ghost moves according to His will.

Since the prophet is called to root out, pull down and destroy, he must be able to see.

> "See, I have this day set thee over the nations and over the kingdoms, to root out, and to pull down, and to destroy, and to throw down, to build, and to plant. Moreover the word of the LORD came unto me, saying, Jeremiah, what seest thou? And I said, I see a rod of an almond tree" (Jeremiah 1:10-11).

FORETELLERS AND FORERUNNERS OF THINGS TO COME

Like John the Baptist, who was the forerunner of Jesus Christ, prophets today are the forerunning voice of things to come. (See Matthew 3:3.)

> Prophets are spiritually graced to go first. (See 1 Corinthians 12:28.)

> "Surely the Lord GOD <u>will do nothing</u>, but he revealeth his secret unto his servants the prophets. The lion hath roared, who will not fear? The Lord GOD hath spoken, who can but prophesy?" (See Amos 3:7-8, Emphasis added.)

PRAYER AND INTERCESSION

Whereas a pastor may take the needs of the people to God in prayer, the prophet will take the Word of the Lord to the people. Prophets often carry lamentations, mourning and woe.

> "And he spread it before me; and it was written within and without: and there was written therein <u>lamentations, and mourning, and woe</u>" (Ezekiel 2:10, Emphasis added).

DELIVERANCE

Deliverance ministry is one of the most common ministries of the prophet. The prophet is called to tear down, destroy, and throw down, before he can build and plant. (See Jeremiah 1:10.) Deliverance ministry will be discussed fully in another class.

DREAMS, VISIONS, REVELATIONS, MYSTERIES

Prophets are stewards of the mysteries of God (1 Corinthians 4:1-2).

"Whereby, when ye read, ye may understand my knowledge in the mystery of Christ which in other ages was not made known unto the sons of men, as it is now revealed unto his holy apostles and prophets by the Spirit" (Ephesians 3:4-5).

FOUNDATIONAL ASCENSION GIFTS

Prophets are not called by God to remain outside the local church, but have been given as foundational gifts to the local church and the Body of Christ. (See Ephesians 2:20.)

Order Gifts

Prophets, similar to apostles, are order gifts. They are foundational and deal with belief systems. When a prophet enters a room or when someone stands in front of him, he immediately knows if anything is out of order. That's the revelation gifting going off inside of him.

Prophets are the most spiritually sensitive of all the five-fold ascension ministry gifts. So if there is anything out of order in the church or out of order in your life, he will pick it up in the spirit. It's not suspicion. Suspicion comes out of the soul through carnal reasoning.

Suspicion is suspecting fault, wrongs or harms with little or no supporting evidence.

The prophetic gift has nothing to do with suspicion or soulish working but operates out of a knowing by the Holy Spirit.

WARRIORS AND REFORMERS

Prophets are called to root out, pull down and to destroy, through intercession prayer, demonic assignments that oppose the Gospel of Jesus Christ. This is evident in the confrontational grace on their lives and is demonstrated in their ability to cause reform.
To reform means to bring about change.

> "See, I have this day set thee over the nations and over the kingdoms, to root out, and to pull down, and to destroy, and to throw down, to build, and to plant" (Jeremiah 1:10).

Prophets will also contend with hard spiritual climates through prayer.

CONTEND WITH FALSE PROPHETS AND DEMONIC GUARDS

False Prophets

> "Now therefore send, and gather to me all Israel unto Mount Carmel, and the prophets of Baal four hundred and fifty, and the prophets of the groves four hundred, which eat at Jezebel's table" (1 Kings 18:19).

Demonic Territorial Guards

Paul and Barnabas confront the sorcerer at Paphos. (See Acts 13:4-12.)

Peter confronted Simon the Sorcerer after Philip's meeting in Samaria. (See Acts 8:13-25.)

TURN HEARTS

One of the primary evidences of a prophet is the urge to turn the hearts of people toward God.

"Behold, I will send you Elijah the prophet before the coming of the great and dreadful day of the LORD: And he shall <u>turn the heart</u> of the fathers to the children, and the heart of the children to their fathers, lest I come and smite the earth with a curse" (Malachi 4:5-6, Emphasis added).

"I have not sent these prophets, yet they ran: I have not spoken to them, yet they prophesied. But if they had stood in my counsel, and had caused my people to hear my words, then they should have <u>turned</u> them from their evil way, and from the evil of their doings" (Jeremiah 23:21-22, Emphasis added).

Prophets challenge vain traditions of men and dead religious activity.

"And think not to say within yourselves, we have Abraham to our father: for I say unto you, that God is able of these stones to raise up children unto Abraham. And now also the ax is laid unto the root of the trees: therefore every tree which bringeth not forth good fruit is hewn down, and cast into the fire" (Matthew 3:9-10).

Prophets place a demand on you to grow and mature.

The prophet John the Baptist declared, "Bring forth therefore fruits meet for repentance" (Matthew 3:8).

CONVICT OF SIN

Prophets carry a grace that convicts people of their sin.

"Cry aloud, spare not, lift up thy voice like a trumpet, and shew my people their transgression, and the house of Jacob their sins" (Isaiah 58:1, Emphasis added).

"And Jonah began to enter into the city a day's journey, and he cried, and said, Yet forty days, and Nineveh shall be overthrown. So the people of Nineveh believed God, and proclaimed a fast, and put on sackcloth, from the greatest of them even to the least of them. For word came unto the king of Nineveh, and he arose from his throne, and he laid his robe from him, and covered him with sackcloth, and sat in ashes. And he caused it to be proclaimed and published through Nineveh by the decree of the king and his nobles, saying, Let neither man nor beast, herd nor flock, taste any thing: let them not feed, nor drink water: But let man and beast be covered with sackcloth, and cry mightily unto God: yea, let them turn every one from his evil way, and from the violence that is in their hands. Who can tell if God will turn and repent, and turn away from his fierce anger, that we perish not? And God saw their works, that they turned from their evil way; and God repented of the evil, that he had said that he would do unto them; and he did it not" (Jonah 3:4-10, Emphasis added).

"Again the word of the LORD came unto me, saying, Son of man, cause Jerusalem to know her abominations" (Ezekiel 16:1-2).

"But if all prophesy, and there come in one that believeth not, or one unlearned, he is convinced of all, he is judged of all: And thus are the secrets of his heart made manifest; and so falling down on his face he will worship God, and report that God is in you of a truth" (1 Corinthians 14:24-25, Emphasis added).

APERCU

In Israel the term "seer" was the title given a prophet. (See 1 Samuel 9:9.)

Since the prophet is called to root out, pull down and destroy, he must be able to see.

Like John the Baptist, who was the forerunner of Jesus Christ, prophets today are the forerunning voice of things to come. (See Matthew 3:3.)

Prophets are stewards of the mysteries of God.

Prophets are the most spiritually sensitive of all the five-fold ascension ministry gifts.

Prophets are called to root out, pull down and to destroy, through intercession prayer, demonic assignments that oppose the Gospel of Jesus Christ.

Prophets contend with false prophets and demonic guards.

One of the primary evidences of a prophet is the urge to turn the hearts of people toward God.

Prophets challenge vain traditions of men and dead religious activity.

Prophets place a demand on you to grow and mature.

NOTES

_____

_____

_____

_____

_____

_____

_____

_____

_____

_____

_____

_____

_____

_____

_____

_____

_____

_____

_____

_____

Reflect & Apply

HALLMARKS OF THE PROPHET

1. What were five names for Old Testament prophets?

    1. _____

    2. _____

    3. _____

    4. _____

    5. _____

2. What are three spiritual burdens that prophets sometime carry?

    1. _____

    2. _____

    3. _____

3. Which ministry is very common for prophets, other than prophecy?

_____

_____

4. What are prophets stewards of?

_____

_____

5. What purpose does Ephesians 2:20 reveal about prophets?

_____

_____

6. What five-fold ascension gift is the most spiritually sensitive?

_____

7. What is the definition of suspicion?

_____

_____

8. What is it that prophets turn?

_____

9. Why do prophets place a demand on believers?

_____

_____

10. What prophet commanded people to produce evidence of their repentance?

_____

NOTES

GLOSSARY

Adulterous prophet: one that is unfaithful and willing to break covenants and agreements.

Announce: to make known by formal notice.

Arrogance: an overbearing pride, exorbitant claims of rank; exalting one's importance to an undue degree.

Chozeh: an open vision resulting in the highest level of prophetic communication.

Col: from the Greek word *collum*, meaning "original dispatch, instrument, deed, seen or heard first."

Comfort: from the Greek word *paramuthia*, meaning "to provide freedom from worry during times of grief, affliction or distress and bringing assurance to the believer."

Commitment: dedication to a longtime course of action.

Corrupt prophet: one who is morally polluted with tainted character, motivations and desires.

Deceit: the deliberate act or practice of deceiving, misleading, tricking, or defrauding.

Desire: from the Greek word *zeloo*, meaning "to burn with zeal."

Edification: from the Greek word *oikodome*, meaning "to build up, establish, and strengthen, to make effective."

Exhortation: from the Greek word *paraklesis*, meaning "a comforting encouragement provided in times of disappointment and affliction resulting in strengthening the resolve of the believer."

Forthtelling prophecy: the simple gift of prophecy is an inspired declaration of the divine will and purpose of God. It is inspired, but not predictive. Its primary use is for edification, exhortation and comfort.

Foretelling prophecy: an inspired declaration that is predictive (speaking of things to come) and directive in it message.

Gift of Faith: One of the nine gifts of the Holy Spirit; having nothing to do with the human will, this gift empowers one to believe for the impossible.

Gifts of Healing: One of the nine gifts of the Holy Spirit; realizing the healing power of God demonstrated through the manifestation of various healings.

Gift of the Working of Miracles: One of the nine gifts of the Holy Spirit; seen when the laws of nature are interpreted. (Time stood still for Joshua, Moses parted the Red Sea, Elijah ran faster than Ahab's chariot, and Jesus turned water into wine, etc.)

Gift of the Word of Wisdom: One of the nine gifts of the Holy Spirit; a verbal prophecy that speaks of the future.

Gift of the Word of Knowledge: One of the nine gifts of the Holy Spirit; a verbal prophecy that speaks of now and the past.

Gift of the Discerning of Spirits: One of the nine gifts of the Holy Spirit; reveals what spirit is speaking, i.e. Holy Spirit, human spirit or demon spirit.

Gift of Prophecy: One of the nine gifts of the Holy Spirit; a supernatural utterance in a known tongue that ministers edification, exhortation and comfort.

Gift of Tongues: One of the nine gifts of the Holy Spirit; a supernatural utterance in an unknown tongue. This gift is demonstrated in the local church assembly when God wants to edify the local church.

Gift of Interpretation of Tongues: One of the nine gifts of the Holy Spirit; the supernatural ability to interpretate the gift of tongues.

Greed: an excessive or insatiable desire to acquire or possess more than what one needs or deserves, especially with respect to material wealth.

Heresies: from the Greek word *hairesis*, meaning "to cause dissension and division through the introduction of a diversity of opinions."

Holiness: freedom from the entanglements of sin.

Imputing: from the Greek word *logizomai*, meaning "to consider the facts and to take them into account when making a decision."

Independence: self-governing, self-reliant, and loyal to no one.

Lie: a false statement deliberately presented as being true; a falsehood, something meant to deceive, or give a wrong impression.

Logizomai: To consider the facts and to take them into account when making a decision.

Morality: biblical standards of conduct.

Moved: from the Greek word *phero*, meaning "to bring forth or to bubble up."

Nabi: an Old Testament name for a prophet.

Obedience: the act of obeying; compliance; words or actions denoting submission to authority.

Power gifts: gifts from the Holy Spirit that do something.

Presumptuous prophet: a presumptuous prophet goes beyond what is right or proper in the scope of prophetic ministry and will prophesy without having received a word from God

Pride: an excessively high opinion of oneself; conceit; haughtiness; superiority lofty air; contempt of others; better than.

Prophetic announcement: the foretelling and predictive operations through prophetic ministry of things to come.

Prophet: a mouthpiece for God.

Prophecy: the Word of God spoken from the mouth of men.

Prophetic protocol: a form of conduct by one who is called as a first dispatch.

Ra'ah: a title given prophets in the Old Testament, a seer.

Reckless prophet: indifferent to others and having an irresponsible disregard for the consequences of their actions.

Proto: a Greek word meaning "to be first."

Protocol: a code of conduct.

Reconciliation: not imputing sins against them.

Revelation gifts: gifts from the Holy Spirit that know something.

Seer: a title given Old Testament prophets.

Seduce: lure, entice, tempt, or beguile, in an effort to mislead.

Spiritual warfare: a method of intercession that uses the authority of the believer to pray against spiritual forces of wickedness in heavenly places.

Suspicion: suspecting fault, wrongs or harms with little or no supporting evidence.

Treacherous: one marked by betrayal that cannot be trusted or relied upon.

Utterance gifts: gifts that say something by revealing information that would be impossible to know without the Holy Spirit making it known.

Watchman: one called to guard, watch, and signal.

REFLECT AND APPLY ANSWER KEY

LESSON 1

1. Unique

2. Distinctiveness

3. Build

4. Rhema word

5. Evangelism

6. Shepherds

7. Disciple

8. Love for people

9. To make students of the word of God

10. A heart for lost souls

11. A hunger for the rhema (prophetic) word of God

12. A desire to build the church

13. Regular occupation

14. Five

15. The work of the apostle (build), prophet (prophesy), evangelists (reach the lost), pastor (love God's people), and teacher (make disciples) that has been imparted to a believer from all five ascension gifts

LESSON 2

1. Sovereign will alone

2. Prophetic dimension

3. Outpouring of the Holy Spirit and prophecy (Acts 2:16-18)

4. Prophecy

5. They were filled with the Holy Spirit, spoke in other tongues and prophesied

6. Gift of tongues and prophecy

7. Miriam, Deborah, Huldah, Isaiah's wife, Anna, Sons and daughters (Acts 2:17-18), Philips four daughters, Women in the Corinthian church

8. Prophecy

9. Burn with zeal

10. Validated

11. Edification, exhortation, comfort

12. Edification, to build up, establish, strengthen, to make effective

LESSON 3

1. Forthtelling and foretelling

2. Forthtelling

3. Forthtelling prophecy, the simple gift of prophecy, is an inspired declaration of the divine will and purpose of God

4. The power gifts, the revelation gifts and the utterance gifts

5. Edify, exhort, comfort

6. Three utterance gifts

7. Gift of tongues and gift of interpretation of tongues

8. Edifies

9. 1 Corinthians 14:31

10. Gift of prophecy, gift of tongues, gift of interpretation of tongues

LESSON 4

1. Jesus gave prophets, the Holy Spirit gave prophecy

2. Amos

3. After a divine unction or urging from the Holy Spirit, during times of worship, through faith, when the Spirit of God comes on you

4. The gift of the Holy Spirit

5. 1 Corinthians 14:32

6. Holy Spirit, Human spirit, evil spirit

7. It should be judged

8. To put to the test for Scriptural accuracy

9. Disregard it

10. Contains "if" statement

LESSON 5

1. Scripture

2. Dreams, Visions, Angelic encounters, Prayer and intercessions, words of knowledge, unctions (urgings and promptings) of the Holy Spirit, trance

3. Presence of the Holy Spirit

4. Stand in the gap and make up the hedge

5. Naaman

6. Elijah received it from God and spoke it to the King of Israel

7. Set man (leader)

8. A desire to pray

9. A love for God's prophetic voice

10. Demonic assignments such as Jezebel spirits, witchcraft, divination, sin, false associations and demonic devices

LESSON 6

1. Manned high towers as look outs for potential danger

2. Stand guard, to keep watch, and say what he sees

3. Watchman

4. Through watching, prayer and intercession

5. Those in authority

6. Warned of a famine. The outcome was provision of a relief gift

LESSON 7

1. Prophet

2. Nabi, Ra'ah, Chozeh

3. Abraham (Genesis 20:7)

4. The word of the Lord coming to the prophet

5. "The word of the Lord came unto me saying."

6. Seer

7. Dreams, visions, angels, or visual prophetic symbolism

8.   Seer or ra'ah prophet

9.   Open visions

10.   Chozeh

LESSON 8

1.   The mind and will of the Lord

2.   She would have a son

3.   "Behold the Lamb of God which taketh away the sin of the world."

4.   Samuel

5.   Dominion authority in his life

6.   The ministry work of Barnabus and Saul

7.   When he laid hands on him and prayed

8.   Prophetic presbytery (1 Timothy 4:14)

9.   Confirmed and activated Paul into ministry

10.   Make known by formal notice

LESSON 9

1.   Extensive training process

2.   Trained by the Holy Spirit

3.   An overbearing pride, exorbitant claims of rank; exalting one's importance to an undue degree

4.   One who is self-governing; self-reliant; loyal to no one

5.   Biblical standard of conduct

6.   The act of obeying; compliance; words or actions denoting submission to authority

7.   Independent prophet

8.   Pride and arrogance

9.   Protocol and perspective

10.   To be first

11.   To be seen or heard first

12.   A form of conduct

LESSON 10

1.   A prediction center

2.   Strongholds

3.   Spiritual warfare, deliverance, prayer and intercession

4.   A method of intercession that uses the authority of the believer to pray against spiritual forces of
         wickedness in heavenly places

5.   Cast out a devil

6.   Ignore the devil

7.   Not ignoring them

8.   Prayer of importunity

9.   Sheep

10.   1. Prayer that doesn't give up – importunity (Luke 18:6-8), 2. Prayer of faith (James 5:15;
         Matthew 21:22; Mark 11:24). 3. Deliverance prayer (Acts 16:18). 4. Binding and loosing
         (Matthew 16:19). 5. Prayer of agreement (Matthew 18:18-20). 6. Praying in the Spirit (Jude 20;
         1 Corinthians 14:4, 14:14-15; Isaiah 28:11-12; Acts 10:46). 7. Fervent effective prayer
         (James 5:16; Romans 12:11; Colossians 4:12). 8. Prayer of consecration and dedication
         (Luke 22:42). 9. Prayer of commitment (1 Peter 5:7). 10. Prayer of worship (Luke 24:52-53;
         Acts 13:1-4). 11. Corporate prayer (Acts 4:23-31). 12. Prayer with groaning and travail
         (Romans 8:26; Isaiah 66:8; Galatians 4:19; Jeremiah 30:6).

LESSON 11

1.   Sin and disobedience to God

2.   Florida hurricanes and California fires

3.   No

4.   No

5.   No

6.   Judged

7.   That "God was in Christ reconciling the world unto himself, not imputing their trespasses unto
         them." (2 Corinthians 5:19)

8.   To consider the facts and to take them into account when making a decision

9.   Bless and curse not

10.   Edification, exhortation, comfort

LESSON 12

1.   A deliberate act or practice of deceiving, misleading, tricking, or defrauding

2.   Merchandiser

3.   No

4.   By their fruit

5.   To curse Israel

6.   Sheep

7.   Greed is an excessive or insatiable desire to acquire or possess more than what one needs or deserves, especially with respect to material wealth

8.   A lie is a false statement deliberately presented as being true; a falsehood, something meant to deceive, or give a wrong impression

9.   Having received a word from God

10.   A reckless prophet is indifferent to others and has an irresponsible disregard for the consequences of their actions

11.   Flattering

LESSON 13

1.   Man of God, Man of the spirit, God's servant, God's messenger, Seer

2.   Lamentation, mourning, woe

3.   Deliverance

4.   Mysteries of God

5.   Foundational belief systems

6.   Prophet

7.   Suspicion

8.   Hearts

9.   To grow and mature in the things of God

10.   John the Baptist

The Author

Jonas Clark is a refreshing voice and a champion in the contemporary church. Jonas served God for more than two decades as a pastor, teacher and evangelist before the Lord called him to his role as an apostle in the end time church.

An evangelist at heart, Jonas travels around the world preaching the Gospel with a bold apostolic anointing. Fortitude and God's grace have taken his ministry into more than 25 countries, where he delivers a message of salvation, healing, deliverance and apostolic reformation. His passion is to win lost souls for Jesus Christ and equip every believer to take the Good News into the harvest fields to fulfill the Great Commission.

Jonas is the founder of The Global Cause Network, an international network of believers and Champion partners united to build a platform for the apostolic voice. He also heads Spirit of Life Ministries, a multi-cultural, non-denominational church in Hallandale Beach, Florida.

Jonas is the publisher of *The Voice* magazine, a media platform for apostolic and prophetic believers.

The Apostolic Equipping Library

Each module of the Apostolic Equipping Library is a 13-week curriculum designed to build a strong foundation in apostolic and prophetic believers.

Christian leaders understand the importance of building solid Biblical truth in believers. The Apostolic Equipping Library has been carefully tailored to guarantee a balanced Scriptural approach in equipping believers for effective ministry.

- Arm your teachers with a solid foundational training curriculum.

- Set the course with training modules designed for presentation in quarterly courses with 13 distinct lessons.

- Organize interactive group studies with chapter summaries that offer relevant discussion points for further exploration.

- Encourage independent study with individual student workbooks that help reinforce the biblical truths imparted during each training session.

- Promote thoughtful examination with Reflect & Apply sections designed to engage the student's mind and spirit.

- Monitor student progress with chapter quizzes.

- Reward each student with a quality Certificate of Completion provided in each workbook.

Please ask about our "Student Pack" discounts designed with ministry cost-savings in mind. We are committed to offering an affordable curriculum for your teachers and students as they discover apostolic-prophetic foundations.

ADDITIONAL APOSTOLIC EQUIPPING LIBRARY MODULES INCLUDE:

Advanced Apostolic Studies

COMING SOON:

Call our offices to inquire about the latest additions to the *Apostolic Equipping Library*. Additional modules on topics including apostolic, prophetic, evangelism, spiritual warfare, healing and deliverance, and the kingship of the believer are in the works.

OTHER BOOKS BY JONAS CLARK INCLUDE:

Jezebel, Seducing Goddess of War

Exposing Spiritual Witchcraft

30 Pieces of Silver

Prophetic Operations

Apostolic Equipping Dimension

Governing Churches & Antioch Apostles

Come Out!

Imaginations, Don't live there!

Rejection is Hell

For more information or to place an order contact:

JONAS CLARK MINISTRIES

27 West Hallandale Beach Blvd. ■ Hallandale Beach, Florida 33009

800.943.6490 ■ www.jonasclark.com

Certificate of Completion

This certifies that

_____

has satisfactorily completed the course in

Xtreme Prophetic STUDIES

from the Apostolic Equipping Library

this _____ *day of* _____ *in the year* _____.

_____

Church / Ministry / School

_____

By Instructor